"I'm not a vegan. I'm not even a vegetarian.
That being said, I love this book. It's packed with creative,
tasty ways to cook with (and make your own) Sriracha sauce.
If you're a fan of the combustible-yet-delicious sauce
known as Sriracha, these recipes are for you."

—MATT INMAN, creator of TheOatmeal.com

"I always have a bottle of Sriracha in my fridge and use it on everything,
so the first thing I did with this book was make my own batch.
Then I proceeded through the chapters, finding ways I never imagined
before to bring this beloved elixir into my cooking. I salute Randy for
daring to go veg, and for writing a book that we carnivores will also enjoy.
He knows better than anyone that Sriracha unites us all."

—SARA KATE GILLINGHAM-RYAN, founding editor, TheKitchn.com

THE VEGGIE-LOVER'S SRIRACHA COOKBOOK

THE **VEGGIE-LOVER'S**
SRIRACHA
COOKBOOK

50 Vegan "Rooster Sauce" Recipes That Pack a Punch

Randy Clemens

PHOTOGRAPHY BY Leo Gong

TEN SPEED PRESS
Berkeley

CONTENTS

BREAKFAST OF CHAMPIONS

MAIN DISHES

DESSERTS AND DRINKS

ACKNOWLEDGMENTS

WORDS CAN'T EXPRESS HOW INCREDIBLE it is to be able to pen yet another Sriracha cookbook. But I guess I've become a legit writer now, so I better figure out how to get some words to express it—that's my job! I feel so privileged to be able to share another collection of awesome recipes with people, especially this batch that I created to honor and celebrate the almighty vegetable.

This couldn't have happened without the help, support, and friendship of so many folks, and I'm glad I get a chance to put some of their names down on paper as my way of recognizing and thanking them for their invaluable contributions. On the family side, big thanks to my mom, Bonnie, for always encouraging my endeavors and leading by the Golden Rule. So much love and gratitude to my Aunt Terri, Uncle Steve, Cousin Kim, Josh, and Miette.

In no particular order, I'm extremely lucky to have friends like Elliot "Gabriel" Weingarten, the darling Cambria Griffith, Gev Kazanchyan (plus Susie and the family, of course!), Josh Lurie, Matt Finkel, Mark Young, Nate Sellergren, Sharaya Olmeda, Tim Herscovitch, Rebecca Fogel, Sergio Salgado, Melinda McKee, and Mark Signaigo.

To Phi and the rest of the Nguyen family, who had no idea that my life flipped the day they introduced me to Sriracha at their house. I'm beyond privileged to know them, and I wish I got to see them more. Thanks also to my heroes the recipe testers, (and also amazing friends): Linzy May Mahoney and family; Madeleine St. Marie; Quarry Girl along with her wonderful husband, Nick; Samantha Loveira; Sandra Hernandez; Kristy and Chris Turner; Sam Edelstein and Erika Barry; and Anya Demianenko and Michael McCoy.

I'm also grateful to those who hosted events for me and/or looked after my general well-being: the Stone Brewing Co. crew (the art/media department, my book pimp Sue, Mr. Cheek, Denise, and the whole rest of you clowns that are gonna be mad I didn't list you by name), Blue Palms Brewhouse and Eagle Rock Brewery (who hosted my first book release party—with a special Sriracha beer!), Tony's Darts Away, Almanac Beer Co., everyone at Port Brewing/the Lost Abbey, Library Alehouse, StudioSchulz.com, and the whole gang from Pacific Coast Harmony.

Thanks to the crew at Ten Speed Press, including Melissa Moore (the greatest editor on earth!), Toni Tajima, Patricia Kelly, Michele Crim, Kara van de Water, Kristin Casemore, Ashley Matuszak, Kelly Snowden, Jenny Burbank, and Ali Slagle. Chloe Rawlins, thanks for making the book look so awesome, with Leo Gong's insanely great photography, and the marvelous food styling of Karen Shinto, plus their illustrious team: prop stylist Carol Hacker and assistants Amanda Hibbert and Agustina Peretta. And lastly, a thank-you to those who've helped fine-tune and advance my writing over the years: Peter Reinhart, Dr. Haut, Ms. Spadafora, Lesley Bargar Suter, Chris Nichols, Greg Koch, Carol Penn-Romine, Nichol Nelson, Karen Young, Eric Mercado, Nancy Zaslavsky, and Amelia Saltsman.

INTRODUCTION

I F*%#ING LOVE VEGETABLES! That, coupled with my addiction to Sriracha, is what ultimately led to the writing of this book. And while I am a firm believer in the righteous virtues of vegetarianism and veganism—of which, there are many—that isn't the focus here. This book isn't about labels; it's not just for vegans or vegetarians. It's for anyone who's incurably passionate about the splendiferous flavors to be had straight from the ground, for anyone who's picked up an eggplant or fennel bulb at the market and dreamed of the possibilities.

I've noticed that over the past decade, cooking and cooking instruction have become decidedly meat-centric, resulting in many home cooks forgetting—or, worse yet, never being taught—how to properly prepare and celebrate the glorious bounty of fruits, vegetables, grains, and legumes that we're fortunate enough to have at our fingertips.

This problem is only compounded when people wrongfully believe that cooking without meat means replacing it with strange, texturized, overly processed soy-based products that have been extruded into shapes vaguely resembling meat, before being breaded and fried. Ugh. You wanna know the truth? I can't stand most of that garbage. It's generally pretty awful tasting, and it usually has very little to do with healthy, fresh ingredients.

And while I've certainly got a place in my kitchen for tempeh and tofu, I don't like my meals to revolve around them. True, you'll find them used within these pages, but only when I feel they can contribute something to the flavor and texture of my beloved veggies, right at the center of my plate.

If you love vegetables too, and a nice spicy kick to boot, let me be the first to congratulate you. You've found the right book. If you've had good vegetables at a friend's house or while dining out but aren't sure how to cook them properly at home, *sweet!* You've found the right book. And if you don't like vegetables, I'm willing to bet it's because you've only had them either overcooked or undercooked your entire life, in which case, you've *finally* found the right book!

Whatever your reasons for giving my cool little book a shot—health, ethical, environmental, economic, a devotion to anything and everything Sriracha-related, or simply curiosity—use these recipes with an open mind. Love them for all that they are, and for all that they aren't. You'll be glad you did!

> If you have any interest in the true implications of including meat, eggs, and dairy in your diet (and you should), I implore you to read *Eating Animals* by Jonathan Safran Foer. It changed my entire worldview and was incredibly nonpreachy, which I appreciate to no end!

SRIRACHA 101

A Tale of Thai Cities

SEATED IN THE CHONBURI PROVINCE of Thailand is Sri Racha, a seaside municipality known for its tropical beach landscape, exotic tiger zoo, delectable seafood restaurants, and affinity for hot chile pastes. Loosely pronounced "see-RAH-chuh," the district is part burgeoning industrial metropolis and part quaint fishing village. Situated about sixty-five miles southeast of Bangkok and with its own port, Sri Racha has attracted many large factories, situated here to avoid the high rent and heavy traffic of the capital city. Besides accommodating the hustle and bustle of big business, Sri Racha has a population of approximately 171,000 and hosts a moderate amount of tourist travel, which helps keep its deeply rooted old Siam culture alive despite the influx of modern machinery.

Clusters of jetties, piers, and dilapidated pontoons protrude out from the shore and into the Gulf of Thailand, keeping hotels, seafood stalls, and other vendors afloat.

Tourists staying a night in town or just passing through en route to some of the eastern seaboard's island destinations, such as Koh Loi or Koh Si Chang, are treated to some of the best fresh seafood money can buy. There isn't a large vegan or vegetarian constituency in Thailand, but some people do choose to follow a plant-based diet, known as *jeh*. While some adhere to it simply as a regime without animal products, in its strictest form the practice also prohibits strongly flavored foods such as onions, garlic, and chiles. (Yikes!) Plus, consumption of alcohol is also a no-no. (Double yikes!)

With many of Sri Racha's residents being immigrant workers from China, Japan, and Korea, the town's restaurants and cuisine have morphed over time to reflect the potpourri of cultures present. But one item that has satiated the people of Sri Racha for many years hasn't changed a bit, and it has managed to remain at the center of the area's eclectic cuisine.

Nám prík Sriracha, a glowing red paste consisting of nothing more than piquant peppers, garlic, vinegar, sugar, and salt, reigns supreme here. The noticeable but certainly not overpowering heat of the chiles and robust pungency of the garlic fuse in the sauce as the vinegar begins pickling and marrying them together. Thai cuisine has traditionally focused on a delicate harmony of four sensations: spicy, salty, sour, and sweet, all of which are gracefully represented in the celebrated crimson condiment, creating the perfect accent for the traditional local fare. Bottled versions, such as Sriracha Panich, became available and gave way to an export market, boosting the sauce's popularity in neighboring countries such as Vietnam, a key step in its voyage to becoming an American obsession.

Coming to America

The Sriracha known to most Americans certainly isn't a far cry from the Thai original, but there are marked differences, and that's just fine with David Tran, creator of the now ubiquitous Tương Ớt Sriracha, or as it is affectionately called by many, "rooster sauce." Tran, who himself was born in Vietnam and is of Chinese ancestry, came to America in the late 1970s as a refugee seeking asylum from the postwar regime. While in Vietnam, Tran had begun growing and selling chile peppers in an attempt to earn a living, but he quickly found that it was a losing proposition due to the low prices paid for fresh chiles. Rather than scrap the plan altogether, he began making chili sauces, which could command a higher return.

After the war, many immigrant groups were viewed as outsiders by the new administration, leaving Tran and his family little choice but to abandon their business and flee their home. Boarding a crowded Taiwanese freighter dubbed *Huy Fong*, Tran left for the United States. After he spent months in a transit camp in Hong Kong, the United States allowed him entry into Boston. Soon thereafter, he moved to Los Angeles and started working there.

Using fifty thousand dollars of family savings after being denied a bank loan, Tran started his chili sauce business in 1980, naming it Huy Fong Foods after the ship that carried him out of Vietnam. With a Chevrolet van, a fifty-gallon electric mixer, and a small shop rented on Spring Street in LA's Chinatown for seven hundred dollars a month, he began selling a spicy Vietnamese-style condiment he called Pepper Saté Sauce to local Asian restaurants and markets. Seeing moderate levels of success, he rolled out several more products, including his Tương Ớt Sriracha in 1983.

Made with bright red jalapeños and utilizing garlic powder rather than fresh garlic, Tran's Sriracha had a more upfront, in-your-face taste that distinguished it from its Thai counterpart. It was bolder and thicker, too. The plastic squeeze bottles, emblazoned with a proud rooster (representing the year of Tran's birth in the Chinese zodiac) and topped with a bright green lid, stood out on restaurant tables and store shelves. The flavor of the sauce was a natural match for Asian cuisine. People outside the Asian community soon took note, gladly embracing a new addition to the drab ketchup, mustard, and mayo condiment trifecta to which many Americans had stoically become accustomed.

By 1986, Tran's operation had outgrown its Chinatown outpost. He moved it to a 68,000-square-foot facility in Rosemead, part of California's San Gabriel Valley, which had its own Asian immigrant community, a perfect market for the sauce. Never advertised, Tương Ớt Sriracha's continued success came solely from its tasty reputation and word of mouth. Coming in at around three dollars for a 17-ounce bottle, the hot sauce was an easy sell to visitors and tourists passing through LA, who often took a bottle or two back home, either for themselves or for friends who had a taste for something spicy.

In 1996, Huy Fong Foods expanded once more, purchasing a shuttered Wham-O factory to facilitate greater production. Most recently, in 2012, the company began a monumental relocation to a forty-million-dollar, 630,000-square-foot build-to-suit factory in Irwindale, California. Their continued success comes as no surprise now that Sriracha has become a pantry staple for many people. With production now exceeding twenty million bottles a year (and the new factory affording them the ability to quintuple that!), it's safe to say that Sriracha has earned its rightful place on tables—and now in cooking pans—across America.

VEGANS, VEGETARIANS, AND CELIACS, OH MY!

A Primer of Sorts

WHEN I SET OUT TO WRITE this book, I wanted to give a shout-out to the vegans who work so hard to do no harm. I myself made the change to vegetarianism shortly after turning in the manuscript for the original *Sriracha Cookbook* back in early 2010 and have since become mostly vegan, though I've been known to exhibit momentary cheesy lapses. But enough about me, and enough about labels.

Whether you're vegan, vegetarian, omnivorous, flexitarian, pescetarian, or of any other dietary persuasion, the purpose of this book isn't to tell you how you should live your life. The recipes contained herein are simply united by three common threads: 1) They all contain copious amounts of Sriracha. 2) They are all fantastic, in my opinion. And 3) they all happen to be vegan, meaning they contain no meat, fish, dairy, eggs, or honey.

Say you simply follow a vegetarian diet or aren't particularly looking to cut out dairy or eggs. No problem. There are notes after some recipes that tell you how you might modify the recipe to include those ingredients. For those who are allergic to gluten (celiacs), can't properly digest it, or simply choose to avoid gluten, most of the recipes are gluten-free, and those that aren't offer suggestions on how to make a gluten-free version. (I know . . . awesome, right?!) Just look for these little logos, **GF** for gluten-free modifications and **V** for vegetarian modifications, throughout the book.

Substitutions and Other Guidelines

In addition to the specific notes on ingredient substitutions that follow some individual recipes, here are some general guidelines to help you get the most out of these recipes and tweak them to fit your dietary needs or principles.

Hidden Animal Products

Alcohol. Because some brewers and vinters filter their products using animal products, vegans and vegetarians alike may want to consult Barnivore.com, an excellent resource for checking whether various beers, wines, and liquors are made without animal products.

Bread and bread crumbs. Most breads are vegetarian, and quite a few are vegan. However, both bread and bread crumbs may contain whey, butter, eggs, and possibly other animal products, so read labels carefully before you purchase.

Pasta. Because some varieties of pasta contain eggs, always check the ingredients before purchasing.

Should You Wish to Use Dairy and Eggs

Butter. Feel free to substitute butter for olive oil or coconut oil except when high-heat frying or deep-fat frying.

Eggs. Whenever you see a mixture of 1 tablespoon ground flaxseeds and 3 tablespoons water being used to create a gel, you can substitute 1 large beaten egg if you like.

Mayonnaise. Feel free to substitute regular mayonnaise for vegan mayonnaise or Flax Mayonnaise (page 17).

Milk. It's fine to use whole milk in place of nondairy milks.

Avoiding Gluten

Miso. While miso is often made solely from soybeans, some brands and varieties do incorporate barley and other non-GF-friendly ingredients. Always check the label.

Soy sauce. If you're using soy sauce rather than Bragg Liquid Aminos, ensure that it's wheat-free—or just use the liquid aminos!

Tempeh. While tempeh is traditionally made from fermented whole soybeans, it does on occasion contain additional ingredients or grains that may not be GF-friendly. Make sure to check the label.

Vegetable stock. Commercial stocks and broths sometimes contain strange ingredients such as hydrolyzed wheat protein, which as you might guess, isn't GF-friendly. If in doubt, you can always make your own stock or use water.

Vinegar. Distilled white vinegar is usually not gluten-free. With apple cider vinegar, some producers make a deceptively marketed "apple cider *flavored* vinegar" that may contain gluten, so check the label (Bragg makes an excellent raw, organic apple cider vinegar that I can't recommend highly enough.)

Hippie Ingredients Explained

Bragg Liquid Aminos. This all-natural gluten-free seasoning made from soybeans is similar in flavor to soy sauce but contains less sodium and is a rich source of sixteen essential and nonessential amino acids, the building blocks of protein. It's available at natural food markets, well-stocked grocery stores, and online.

Coconut milk. When the recipes in this book call for coconut milk, I'm referring to the whole-fat canned variety, not the reduced-fat version or the nondairy milk in cartons.

Flaxseeds. In addition to being a rich source of heart-healthy omega-3 fatty acids, flaxseeds form a gel when mixed with water, creating a texture that's perfect for use as an egg substitute or as a base for a vegan mayo. Flaxseeds are available ground or whole at natural food markets, well-stocked grocery stores, and online. Store them in the refrigerator.

Grade B maple syrup. Make sure you get the real deal when you buy maple syrup. Avoid anything labeled "maple-flavored syrup," "table syrup," or "pancake syrup"; they're nothing more than high-fructose corn syrup with caramel color, artificial flavor, a bunch of other Frankenfoods, and possibly some natural flavor if you're lucky. Real maple syrup, on the other hand, is one of nature's most delightful treats. Grade A is a little lighter in color than Grade B, since most of the so-called impurities are filtered out. However, those "impurities" impart some of the most excellent flavors, even if the syrup isn't as crystal clear. If the price scares you off, use raw agave nectar instead; it has a similar taste and is often only half the cost.

Kombu. Kombu is a type of seaweed typically used in Japanese cooking, where it's prized for the rich umami quality it possesses. It can be found in natural food stores, Asian markets, and online.

Miso. (Shown on page 13, top.) Hailing from Japan, miso is a fermented paste typically made from soybeans. Some varieties include ingredients that contain gluten, such as barley, so if that's a concern for you, be sure to check the label. In this book, I only call for yellow or white miso, which contribute umami, saltiness, and a slightly cheesy flavor to the end product.

Nondairy milk. There's always that clever person that wants to make the joke "So, how do you milk an almond, Randy?" Yes, yes, very funny. I'm laughing inside. No, really. I am! I hadn't heard that one before! Anyway, the wide variety of nondairy milk substitutes available include versions made from soybeans, almonds, rice, hazelnuts, and hemp, to name the most common. It's usually made by steeping the base ingredient in water for a prescribed amount of time, then blending and straining to yield a liquid with some of the flavor and nutrients of the base without the solids. For the recipes in this book, I leave the variety to your preference unless specifically noted. No matter which "milk" you go with, make sure to use an unsweetened, unflavored variety.

Nutritional yeast flakes. An inactive yeast that is rich in B vitamins and protein, nutritional yeast contributes an excellent cheesy, somewhat nutty flavor to dishes and is essential for creating any sort of nondairy cheeze base contained within these hallowed pages. (All the cool kids call it "nooch," but you already knew that, didn't ya, cool kid? Yeah, I thought so!) Try it sprinkled on baked potatoes, grilled corn, pasta, popcorn, or, just about any savory food.

Tempeh. (Shown opposite, bottom right.) Made from cultured and fermented whole soybeans pressed into blocks, usually rectangular in shape, tempeh is plenty tasty when marinated and then roasted, grilled, or otherwise cooked in its block form. And when crumbled, its texture allows it to excel as a substitute for ground meat. Some varieties do incorporate grains (or beans other than soybeans), so if gluten is an issue for you, be sure to check the list of ingredients.

Tofu. (Shown opposite, bottom left.) Made by coagulating soy milk and then pressing it to expel excess liquid from the curds, tofu is an excellent source of vegetable protein and works well as a blank canvas for flavor. While I haven't used it excessively in this book, opting instead for fresh, unprocessed ingredients wherever possible, there are instances where I feel it is a complementary ingredient, whether for flavor, appearance, texture, or some combination thereof.

Vegan mayonnaise. A variety of brands and types of vegan mayonnaise are available at natural food stores and well-stocked grocery stores. Look for it both in the cold case and on the shelves alongside conventional mayonnaise. Or, if you'd like to make your own, you can whip up a batch of Flax Mayonnaise (page 17).

Vegan shortening and vegan butter. A couple of the recipes call for "nonhydrogenated vegetable shortening," which sounds just about as healthy as eating a tub of shoe polish. The store-bought stuff is only a little questionable in my book, but if you want to make your own with more wholesome ingredients, there is a way. Mattie Hagedorn, vegan blogger extraordinaire, went super scientific and figured out an awesome way to make damn good vegan butter, and it only requires a few slightly uncommon (but completely natural) ingredients that are relatively easy to obtain. His (not-so-)secret recipe can be found via a link I've posted at SrirachaBook.com/extras.

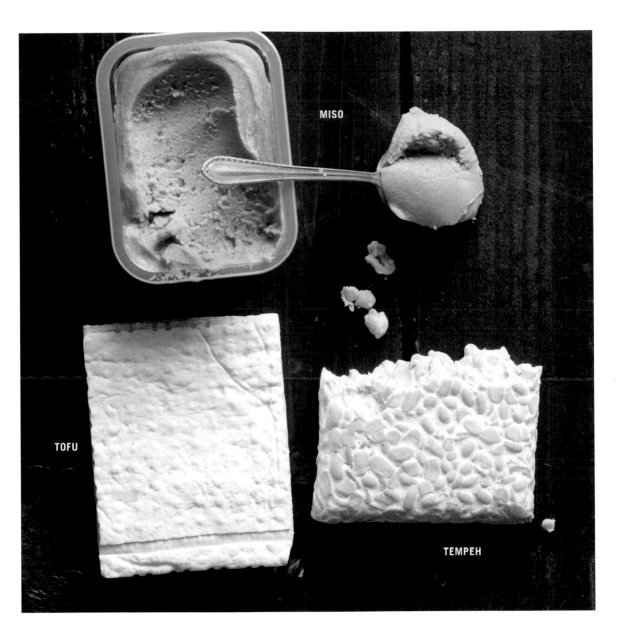

MISO

TOFU

TEMPEH

SAUCES, STARTERS, AND SNACKS

HOMEMADE SRIRACHA

Why on earth would you want to make your own Sriracha? I mean, the bottled stuff is already amazing, and it's actually cheaper to buy than it is to make. Um, because you can! Plus, it's delicious and easy to make, and there's that cool sense of pride that comes with the DIY approach. That's something money just can't buy. **MAKES ABOUT 2 CUPS**

1³/₄ pounds red jalapeño chiles, stemmed and halved lengthwise

3 cloves garlic, peeled

2 tablespoons garlic powder

2 tablespoons granulated sugar

1 tablespoon kosher salt

1 tablespoon light brown sugar

¹/₂ cup distilled white vinegar

Water if needed

In a food processor, combine the jalapeños, garlic, garlic powder, granulated sugar, salt, and brown sugar. Pulse until a coarse puree forms. Transfer to a glass jar, seal, and store at room temperature for 7 days, stirring daily.

After 1 week, pour the mixture into a small saucepan. Stir in the vinegar and bring to a boil over medium-high heat. Lower the heat and simmer gently for 5 minutes. Let cool to room temperature, then transfer to a food processor and process for 2 to 3 minutes. If the mixture is too thick to blend well, add a bit of water.

Pass the mixture through a fine-mesh strainer. Press on the solids with the back of a spoon to squeeze out every last bit of goodness. Taste and adjust the flavor and consistency to suit your taste by adding additional garlic powder, granulated sugar, salt, vinegar, or water if desired. Use immediately or store in a glass jar in the refrigerator for up to 6 months.

SRIRACHA AIOLI

This spicy mayo is great on sandwiches, wraps, French fries, or roasted corn (see sidebar, page 106).
MAKES ABOUT 1 CUP

2/3 cup vegan mayonnaise or Flax Mayonnaise (see below)

1/3 cup Sriracha

1 large clove garlic, minced

1 tablespoon freshly squeezed lime juice

In a bowl, mix all the ingredients. Add more lime juice for a thinner consistency if desired. Use immediately or store in the refrigerator for up to 2 weeks.

FLAX MAYONNAISE

Flaxseeds act as a great healthy emulsifier for this nifty, thrifty vegan mayo. **MAKES ABOUT 1 CUP**

1 tablespoon ground flaxseeds

3 tablespoons water

2 tablespoons freshly squeezed lemon juice

1 teaspoon dry mustard

1 teaspoon fine sea salt

1 teaspoon sugar

Pinch of cayenne pepper

1 cup vegetable oil

In a small bowl, mix the flaxseeds and water and let sit for several minutes, until a gel forms. Transfer to a food processor and add the lemon juice, mustard, salt, sugar, cayenne, and 1/4 cup of the oil. Process until thoroughly combined. With the processor running, slowly add the remaining 3/4 cup of oil, and continue processing until thick like, well, mayonnaise. Taste and season with additional salt or lemon juice if desired. Use immediately or store in the refrigerator for up to 1 month.

SRIRANCHA DRESSING AND DIP

This tasty twist on ranch dressing is great on iceberg wedge salad, crudités, pizza, or baked potatoes.
MAKES ABOUT 1 CUP

$3/4$ cup raw whole cashews, soaked in water for 2 hours

$1/4$ cup unsweetened nondairy milk

$1/4$ cup Sriracha

1 tablespoon freshly squeezed lemon juice

2 cloves garlic, peeled

1 tablespoon chopped fresh flat-leaf parsley

1 tablespoon chopped fresh chives, or 1 teaspoon dried

1 tablespoon chopped fresh dill, or 1 teaspoon dried

Salt and freshly ground black pepper

Drain the cashews. Put them in a food processor or high-speed blender and add the nondairy milk, Sriracha, lemon juice, and garlic. Puree until very smooth, pausing once or twice to scrape down the sides with a rubber spatula. Add the parsley, chives, and dill and pulse until combined. Season with salt and pepper to taste. Transfer to an airtight container and refrigerate for at least 2 hours before serving. Stored in the refrigerator, it will keep for up to 1 week.

V Feel free to substitute $1/4$ cup buttermilk for the nondairy milk.

SRIRACHA KETCHUP

This ketchup with a kick is great on burgers, French fries, hash browns, or grilled cheeze sandwiches.
MAKES ABOUT 1 CUP

$3/4$ cup ketchup

$1/4$ cup Sriracha

1 tablespoon minced fresh flat-leaf parsley (optional)

In a bowl, mix all the ingredients. Use immediately or store in the refrigerator for up to 2 months.

SRIRACHA PESTO

This zesty vegan pesto is great on pasta (hot or cold), pizza, crudités, panini, grilled tofu, mashed potatoes, or roasted corn (see page 106). **MAKES ABOUT 1 CUP**

1/4 cup raw walnut halves
1 large clove garlic, peeled
1/2 cup firmly packed spinach leaves
1/4 cup firmly packed arugula leaves
6 large fresh basil leaves
2 tablespoons nutritional yeast flakes
2 tablespoons Sriracha
1 tablespoon freshly squeezed lemon juice
1/4 cup extra-virgin olive oil
Salt and freshly ground black pepper

In a food processor or high-speed blender, combine the walnuts and garlic and pulse until finely chopped. Add the spinach, arugula, basil, nutritional yeast, Sriracha, and lemon juice and process until a coarse paste forms. With the processor running, slowly add the oil through the feed tube. Season with salt and pepper to taste. Use immediately or store in the refrigerator for up to 1 week.

V Feel free to substitute 2 tablespoons grated Parmigiano-Reggiano cheese for the nutritional yeast flakes.

COCK SAUCE CASHEW CHEEZE

This cheeze makes a great dip and spread and is useful in a multitude of recipes. It has a texture akin to fresh chèvre and can be used in place of cream cheese or ricotta. Personalize it by experimenting with your favorite spices or minced herbs. Try it in lasagna, jalapeño peppers, or Stuffed Sriracha 'Shrooms (page 28) for starters. **MAKES ABOUT 1¹/₂ CUPS**

1 cup raw whole cashews, soaked in water for 2 hours

1 small red bell pepper, quartered

3 tablespoons nutritional yeast flakes

3 tablespoons Sriracha

1 tablespoon freshly squeezed lemon juice

2 cloves garlic, peeled

Water if needed

Salt and freshly ground black pepper

Drain the cashews. Put them in a food processor or high-speed blender and add the bell pepper, nutritional yeast, Sriracha, lemon juice, and garlic. Puree until smooth, pausing once or twice to scrape down the sides with a rubber spatula. With the processor running, drizzle in water for a thinner consistency if desired. Season with salt and pepper to taste. Transfer to an airtight container and refrigerate for at least 2 hours before serving. Stored in the refrigerator, it will keep for 1 week.

V Feel free to use 1 (8-ounce) package cream cheese, softened, or 8 ounces fresh chèvre in place of the cashews and nutritional yeast.

SRIRACHA-CUCUMBER HUMMUS

Hummus works well as a blank canvas, allowing you to add whatever ingredients and flavors you like. I discovered this particular combination while working at Stone Brewing Co., as it was often served in their bistro. The cucumber adds a light, refreshing zip that plays unbelievably well with the fiery force that is Sriracha. **MAKES ABOUT 2 CUPS**

1 English cucumber, peeled

1³/4 cups cooked garbanzo beans, or 1 (15-ounce) can, drained

4 cloves garlic, peeled

¹/4 cup raw tahini

3 tablespoons Sriracha

Juice of 1 lemon

2 tablespoons extra-virgin olive oil, plus more for drizzling

1 tablespoon ground cumin

2 teaspoons smoked paprika

Salt and freshly ground black pepper

Cut the cucumber into quarters. Put three of the quarters in a food processor or high-speed blender and add the garbanzo beans, garlic, tahini, Sriracha, lemon juice, oil, cumin, and paprika. Process until smooth. Season with salt and pepper to taste.

Transfer to a serving bowl and use a spoon to form a small divot in the center. Dice the remaining cucumber and place it in the divot. Drizzle a bit of olive oil over the top. Transfer to an airtight container and refrigerate for at least 2 hours before serving. Stored in the refrigerator, leftovers will keep for up to 1 week.

IN THE RAW Not long ago, I discovered the joy of sprouting garbanzo beans, which allows you to eat them raw, preserving more of their natural nutrients. Plus, they lend an awesome texture to hummus. Want to sprout your own? Head to SrirachaBook.com/extras for directions.

SRIRACHA-MANGO GUACAMOLE

I've long served both guacamole and my (semi)famous mango salsa with tortilla chips. One day I wondered what would happen if I made a hybrid of the two dips, and deliciousness was born. The addition of Sriracha wasn't exactly rocket science, but it does taste absolutely brilliant. Besides being an excellent dip for chips or crudités, it also makes a tasty topping for grilled tofu, and of course goes well in tacos, burritos, and other Mexican fare. **MAKES ABOUT 2 CUPS**

3 large, ripe Hass avocados
Juice of 2 large limes
1 large mango, diced
1/4 cup diced red onion
1/4 cup chopped fresh cilantro
1/4 cup Sriracha
2 cloves garlic, minced
1 1/2 teaspoons ground cumin
Salt and freshly ground black pepper
Cilantro sprigs, for garnish

Cut the avocados in half, remove the pits, and scoop the flesh into a bowl. Add the lime juice. Using a fork, mash the avocado until relatively smooth. Add most of the mango (reserving a small amount for garnish) and the onion, cilantro, Sriracha, garlic, and cumin, mixing well. Season with salt and pepper to taste. Cover with plastic wrap, pressing the plastic onto the surface of the guac to help prevent browning. Refrigerate for at least 30 minutes. Just before serving, taste and adjust the seasoning if desired. Garnish with the reserved mango and cilantro sprigs and serve immediately. Stored in the refrigerator with plastic wrap pressed onto the surface, leftovers will keep for 3 days.

BURNING THAI BRUSCHETTA

This is definitely a fun appetizer to serve up. At first glance, it looks similar to traditional Italian bruschetta, but at first bite, the ginger and Thai basil tell your taste buds that they're in for something different. And then the Sriracha kicks in. Surprise! **MAKES 4 TO 6 SERVINGS**

1 large lime

8 ounces cherry tomatoes, halved lengthwise

3 green onions, white and green parts, sliced on the diagonal

2 tablespoons Sriracha

2 teaspoons Bragg Liquid Aminos or low-sodium soy sauce

1 teaspoon grated fresh ginger

1 teaspoon light brown sugar

8 large fresh Thai basil leaves, thinly sliced

4 large cloves garlic, peeled

Salt and freshly ground black pepper

1 baguette

Extra-virgin olive oil, for drizzling

Preheat the oven to 350°F.

Zest and juice the lime, then finely mince the zest. In a large nonreactive bowl, mix the lime juice and zest along with the tomatoes, green onions, Sriracha, liquid aminos, ginger, brown sugar, and basil. Mince 3 cloves of the garlic and stir them in. Season lightly with salt and pepper. Cover and let sit at room temperature. (This can be prepared up to 1 day ahead and stored in the refrigerator.)

Meanwhile, slice the baguette 1 inch thick on the diagonal. Arrange the slices in a single layer on a baking sheet. Drizzle lightly with olive oil. Bake for about 4 minutes, until golden but not quite brown. Remove from the oven and, while still warm, rub the remaining clove of garlic across the top of each slice. The coarse texture of the toasted bread will act like a grater, getting little flecks of garlicky glory onto each piece.

Taste the tomato mixture and season with additional salt and pepper if desired. Transfer to a serving bowl and serve alongside the toasted baguette, allowing diners to spoon on their own tomato topping.

GF Gluten-free sandwich bread can be substituted for the baguette. Simply cut 4 or 5 slices in quarters and toast as directed. Alternatively, you can use gluten-free crackers. If using crackers, mince the fourth clove of garlic along with the other three and add it to the tomato mixture since you won't need to "grate" it.

SRIRACHA MUHAMMARA

You know those moments that are burned into your memory forever, like the first time you heard Earth, Wind & Fire belt out "September," or when you finally got to make out with the person you pined for all through high school? Friggin' awesome, right? Well, that's how I feel about my first *muhammara* experience. I was working under chef Michael Ruiz at the late LA restaurant Bistro Verdu, and when he introduced me to the wonderfully smoky and tangy Middle Eastern dip, I instantly fell in love with it. **MAKES ABOUT 1½ CUPS**

1 cup raw walnut halves
1 roasted red bell pepper
4 cloves garlic, peeled
3 tablespoons Sriracha
2 tablespoons pomegranate molasses
(see sidebar at right)
1 tablespoon smoked paprika
Salt and freshly ground black pepper

In a food processor or high-speed blender, combine the walnuts, bell pepper, garlic, Sriracha, pomegranate molasses, and paprika. Process until mostly smooth but still with lots of small, chunky bits of walnut. Transfer to an airtight container and refrigerate for at least 2 hours. Season with salt and pepper to taste just before serving. Stored in the refrigerator, leftovers will keep for 1 week.

POMEGRANATE MOLASSES
Pomegranate molasses is a sweet-and-sour reduction of pomegranate juice that can be found online and in Middle Eastern markets. If you're unable to find it or would just like to be cool and make your own, simply combine 2 cups pomegranate juice, ¼ cup sugar, and the juice of 1 lemon in a nonreactive saucepan over very low heat. Cook, stirring occasionally, until reduced to a thick syrup, about 1 hour. Use immediately or store in the refrigerator for up to 6 months.

SRIRACHA CAPONATA

O eggplant, how do I love thee? I can't even begin to count the ways, but let caponata stand as a shining example of just why I love you so. Sour, sweet, slightly salty, and now—with the addition of Sriracha—spicy, too. Although caponata is typically served as a topping on baguette slices or crostini, it's also great in panini or over couscous, pasta, grain salads, or grilled tofu. MAKES 4 TO 6 SERVINGS

$^1/_2$ cup extra-virgin olive oil

1 large red onion, diced large

2 Japanese eggplants, unpeeled, diced large

1 red bell pepper, diced large

1 stalk celery, diced large

$^1/_4$ cup raisins

4 cloves garlic, minced

1 (14-ounce) can tomato puree

$^1/_4$ cup pitted kalamata olives

$^1/_4$ cup Sriracha

$^1/_4$ cup apple cider vinegar

1 tablespoon sugar

1 tablespoon nonpareil capers (optional)

2 tablespoons chopped fresh flat-leaf parsley, plus more for garnish

Salt and freshly ground black pepper

Toasted pine nuts (see sidebar, page 53), for garnish (optional)

Heat the oil in a cast-iron or nonstick skillet over medium-high heat. Add the onion and sauté until softened, 5 to 7 minutes. Add the eggplants, bell pepper, and celery and sauté until softened, about 5 minutes. Add the raisins and garlic and sauté just until the garlic is fragrant, about 30 seconds. Stir in the tomato puree, olives, Sriracha, vinegar, sugar, and capers. Bring to a boil, then immediately lower the heat and simmer gently until the sauce has thickened, about 20 minutes.

Remove from the heat and stir in the parsley. Season with salt and pepper to taste. The dish should have a nice balance of sweet and sour, so taste and add more vinegar or sugar as desired. Serve warm, at room temperature, or chilled, garnished with parsley and pine nuts. Stored in the refrigerator, leftovers will keep for 1 week.

STUFFED SRIRACHA 'SHROOMS

There is perhaps no hot hors d'oeuvre finer than well-made stuffed mushrooms, especially when they're this easy to put together. If you're making them for a party, you can assemble them the day before and refrigerate overnight. Simply let them come to room temperature, drizzle with olive oil, and bake when ready to serve. Your guests will, like, totally trip out on how good they are, maaaan. MAKES 4 TO 6 SERVINGS AS AN APPETIZER

24 cremini or button mushrooms
3 tablespoons extra-virgin olive oil
   Salt and freshly ground black pepper
2 cloves garlic, minced
1 cup Cock Sauce Cashew Cheeze (page 20)
   Thinly sliced fresh basil leaves, for garnish

Remove the stems from the mushrooms. Chop the stems finely. Heat 1¹/₂ tablespoons of the oil in a cast-iron or nonstick skillet over medium heat. Add the mushroom stems and season lightly with salt and pepper. Sauté until the mushrooms have given off their moisture and are slightly browned, about 5 minutes. Add the garlic and sauté just until fragrant, about 30 seconds. Transfer to a bowl and let cool to room temperature.

Preheat the oven to 375°F.

Add the cheeze to the mushroom stems and mix well. Arrange the mushroom caps, gill side up, on a nonstick or parchment-lined rimmed baking sheet. Season lightly with salt and pepper. Fill each mushroom with a generous heap of the cheeze mixture. (If making in advance, stop here and cover and refrigerate for up to 1 day.)

Drizzle the remaining 1¹/₂ tablespoons oil over the mushrooms. Bake for 25 to 30 minutes, until the mushroom caps begin to wrinkle and give off their moisture. Garnish with basil and serve immediately.

Ⓥ Replace the cheeze with one (8-ounce) block of cream cheese, softened, mixed with 1 egg yolk, 1 tablespoon freshly squeezed lemon juice, ¹/₂ cup grated Parmigiano-Reggiano cheese, 3 tablespoons Sriracha, and 2 cloves garlic, minced.

NOT YOUR MAMA'S PARTY MIX

Well, it's not *my* mama's party mix, anyway. Every December, my mom would break out the big roasting pan and make insane quantities of Chex mix to give as gifts to friends and family (though I ate way more than my rationed share, much to my mom's chagrin). It was crazy addictive, and with a few simple adjustments, now it's vegan. The awesome addition of Sriracha only makes it that much more like snack crack—and I'm totally alright with that. **MAKES ABOUT 15 CUPS; ANYWHERE BETWEEN 8 AND 16 SERVINGS**

3 cups wheat squares cereal (such as Wheat Chex)

3 cups rice squares cereal (such as Rice Chex)

3 cups corn squares cereal (such as Corn Chex)

3 cups toasted oat cereal (such as Cheerios)

2 cups pretzel sticks

1 (10-ounce) can cocktail peanuts

1 (10-ounce) can fancy mixed nuts

1 cup melted coconut oil, extra-virgin olive oil, or a mixture of the two

1/2 cup Sriracha

3 tablespoons Bragg Liquid Aminos or low-sodium soy sauce

2 tablespoons garlic powder

Preheat the oven to 250°F.

In a very large roasting pan, gently mix the cereals, pretzels, peanuts, and mixed nuts. In a measuring cup, mix the coconut oil, Sriracha, liquid aminos, and garlic powder. Drizzle over the cereal mixture while stirring gently, then continue stirring until everything is evenly coated.

Bake for 1 hour, stirring every 15 minutes. Let cool slightly before serving. Stored in an airtight container at room temperature, it will keep for 1 month (as if!).

GF Substitute more rice or corn cereal for the wheat squares. Toasted oats cereal obviously contains oats (duh!), which some folks who are sensitive to gluten can't tolerate or choose to avoid. Gluten-free brands—such as Nature's Path Whole-O's—work great.

SOUTHEAST MEETS SOUTHWEST LETTUCE CUPS

I *love* lettuce cups. Anytime you can get people reaching for the same plate in the center of the table, you're guaranteed a lively conversation. Plus, the heat of the filling mixes with the cool crunch of the lettuce to create a fun juxtaposition. This version ups the contrast ante with ingredients from both Southeast Asia, and the US Southwest. If you'd like to serve them with a dipping sauce, check out the recipe for vegan *nước chấm* (see sidebar, page 77) or Sriracha Satay Sauce (page 57). **MAKES 4 TO 6 SERVINGS**

2 (8-ounce) packages plain tempeh, crumbled

Juice of 2 limes

¹/₄ cup Bragg Liquid Aminos or low-sodium soy sauce

¹/₄ cup Sriracha

4 cloves garlic, minced

2 tablespoons grated fresh ginger

3 tablespoons extra-virgin olive oil

4 green onions, white and green parts, sliced on the diagonal

1¹/₂ cups cooked black beans, or 1 (15-ounce) can, drained

1 cup fresh or frozen, thawed corn kernels

1 cup diced jicama

¹/₄ cup chopped fresh cilantro

1 head iceberg, Boston, or Bibb lettuce, leaves separated

Put the tempeh in a large bowl or ziplock bag. In a separate bowl, whisk together the lime juice, liquid aminos, Sriracha, garlic, and ginger. Pour over the tempeh and mix until evenly coated. Let marinate for 20 to 30 minutes.

Meanwhile, heat the oil in a cast-iron or nonstick skillet over medium-high heat. Add the green onions and sauté just until fragrant, about 30 seconds. Add the tempeh and its marinade, then stir in the beans, corn, and jicama. Cover and cook until heated through, about 7 minutes. Remove from the heat, stir in the cilantro, and serve immediately in a large bowl alongside the lettuce leaves. Allow your dining guests to scoop the hot mixture onto the lettuce leaves, forming a kind of leafy taco. Dunk into your dipping sauce of choice before each bite, and enjoy!

SOUPS
AND
STEWS

FIVE-ALARM BLACK BEAN SOUP WITH CILANTRO-COCONUT CREMA

Black bean soup is one of my favorite comfort foods, and I've long enjoyed it with a dollop of sour cream or crème fraîche. But, in reevaluating my gustatory choices, I decided to create a mock sour cream using coconut, especially since coconut works so well with black beans in Caribbean-style cuisine. **MAKES 4 TO 6 SERVINGS**

Cilantro-Coconut Crema

- 1 (14-ounce) can coconut milk (*not* the low-fat or light variety)
- Juice of 1 to 2 limes
- 2 tablespoons chopped fresh cilantro
- 1 tablespoon white or yellow miso (optional)
- 1/2 teaspoon kosher salt

Soup

- 2 tablespoons extra-virgin olive oil
- 1 large red onion, diced
- 2 stalks celery, diced
- 1 red bell pepper, diced
- 3 cloves garlic, minced
- 2 tablespoons ground cumin
- 1 teaspoon ground allspice or ground cloves
- 2 bay leaves
- 4 cups vegetable stock
- 3 1/2 cups cooked black beans, or 2 (15-ounce) cans, undrained
- 1/4 cup Sriracha, plus more for garnish
- Salt and freshly ground black pepper

To make the crema, refrigerate the can of coconut milk for at least 4 hours. Open the can and scoop out all the creamy goodness that's solidified in there into a bowl, leaving any liquid behind in the can. Add in the juice of 1 lime, cilantro, miso, and salt. Mix until smooth, with the consistency of sour cream. Taste and season with more salt or lime juice if desired. Transfer to an airtight container and refrigerate until serving time.

To make the soup, heat the oil in a large Dutch oven or soup pot over medium-high heat. Add the onion, celery, and bell pepper and sauté until the vegetables start to soften and brown slightly, about 8 minutes. Add the garlic, cumin, allspice, and bay leaves and sauté just until the garlic is fragrant, about 30 seconds. Pour in 1 cup of the stock to deglaze the pan, using a wooden spoon to scrape up all the stubborn, tasty brown bits. Stir in the remaining 3 cups of stock, the beans, and the Sriracha. Bring to a boil, then immediately lower the heat and simmer gently until the soup has thickened, about 20 minutes.

Discard the bay leaves. Season with salt and pepper to taste. (For a thicker consistency, ladle 2 cups of the soup into a food processor or high-speed blender. Place a folded towel over the lid and hold the towel and lid down to prevent the hot liquid from escaping. Blend until smooth, then stir back into the pot.) Serve immediately, topped with a dollop of the crema and garnished with a healthy drizzle of Sriracha. Stored in the refrigerator, leftovers will keep for 1 week.

Ⓥ When making the crema, feel free to substitute 3/4 cup sour cream for the coconut milk, lime juice, miso, and salt. Simply stir the chopped cilantro into the sour cream. Just be aware that you'll miss out on that awesome coconut flavor! A little Cotija cheese crumbled on top would also be delicious.

ZIPPY ZUCCHINI ZUPPA WITH ASPARAGUS AND CANNELLINI BEANS

Cannellini beans (aka white kidney beans) are one of my favorite things on earth. Sure, they're pretty similar to other white beans—and great northern or navy beans can certainly be used interchangeably with them in this recipe—but there's something about their delicious flavor and their large size that commands respect. In this soup, adding a variety of verdant veggies and several spoonfuls of scarlet Sriracha takes them over the top. See photo on page 32. **MAKES 4 TO 6 SERVINGS**

2 tablespoons extra-virgin olive oil

1 large red onion, diced

2 stalks celery, diced

1 large carrot, diced

1 large zucchini, quartered lengthwise and sliced

3 cloves garlic, minced

3 sprigs thyme, stemmed and minced

2 bay leaves

4 cups vegetable stock

3^1/$_2$ cups cooked cannellini beans, or 2 (15-ounce) cans, undrained

^{1}/$_4$ cup Sriracha, plus more for garnish

1 bunch asparagus, trimmed and quartered crosswise

1 teaspoon grated lemon zest

Juice of 1 lemon

Salt and freshly ground black pepper

Chopped fresh flat-leaf parsley, for garnish

Heat the oil in a large Dutch oven or soup pot over medium-high heat. Add the onion, celery, and carrot and sauté until the vegetables start to soften and brown slightly, about 8 minutes. Add the zucchini, garlic, thyme, and bay leaves and sauté just until the garlic is fragrant, about 30 seconds. Pour in 1 cup of the stock and deglaze the pan with a wooden spoon. Stir in the remaining 3 cups of stock, the beans, and the Sriracha. Bring to a boil, then immediately lower the heat, cover, and simmer gently for 15 minutes.

Stir in the asparagus and cook, stirring occasionally, until the soup has thickened and the beans and vegetables are soft, about 5 minutes. Discard the bay leaves. Stir in the lemon juice and zest, then season with salt and pepper to taste. Serve immediately, garnished with parsley and a healthy drizzle of Sriracha. Stored in the refrigerator, leftovers will keep for 1 week.

SRIRACHILI NON CARNE

You see what I did there? Sriracha + Chili = Srirachili. And *non carne*? It's a play on *con carne*! Ha! Whew, I crack myself up! To take this dish into the stratosphere, serve it garnished with corn chips, chopped red onion, and chopped cilantro or parsley. **MAKES 4 TO 6 SERVINGS**

2 tablespoons extra-virgin olive oil

1 large red onion, diced

1 green bell pepper, diced

2 (8-ounce) packages tempeh, crumbled

2 tablespoons Bragg Liquid Aminos or low-sodium soy sauce

2 cloves garlic, minced

1^1/$_2$ tablespoons ground cumin

1 tablespoon chili powder

2 teaspoons smoked paprika

2 bay leaves

1 tablespoon tomato paste

^{1}/$_4$ cup Sriracha

12 fluid ounces dark beer (porter or stout)

1 (14^1/$_2$-ounce) can stewed tomatoes

1^3/$_4$ cups cooked red kidney beans, or 1 (15-ounce) can, undrained

Salt and freshly ground black pepper

Heat the oil in a large Dutch oven or soup pot over medium-high heat. Stir in the onion and bell pepper. Lower the heat to medium and cook, stirring occasionally, until the onion begins to turn golden brown, 15 to 20 minutes.

Add the tempeh and cook, stirring occasionally and breaking up any large clumps, until it begins to brown, about 5 minutes. Add the liquid aminos, garlic, cumin, chili powder, paprika, bay leaves, tomato paste, and Sriracha and cook, stirring constantly, for about 1 minute. Pour in half of the beer to deglaze the pan, using a wooden spoon to scrape up the tasty brown bits. Stir in the remaining beer, the tomatoes and their juices, and the beans. Bring to a boil, then immediately lower the heat and simmer gently until the chili has thickened, about 20 minutes. Discard the bay leaves. Season with salt and pepper to taste. Stored in the refrigerator, leftovers will keep for 1 week.

Ⓥ Sour cream and/or grated Cheddar would be delightful toppings.

GF If you're able to track down a dark, gluten-free beer that you enjoy, by all means, use it. Alternatively, you can use gluten-free vegetable stock or water.

FIERY PHỞ CHAY

When I posted a picture of vegan *phở* on *The Sriracha Cookbook*'s Facebook page, some Internet troll felt compelled to comment that it wasn't *phở* because there was no meat. I politely replied by drawing attention to the fact that many Buddhists in Southeast Asia and around the globe adhere to vegetarian diets, and they're more than happy to enjoy said soup without meat, thank you very much! MAKES 4 TO 6 SERVINGS

Broth

2 large yellow onions, cut into 1-inch-thick rings

8 cups water

1/2 cup Sriracha

1/4 cup Bragg Liquid Aminos or low-sodium soy sauce

3 (4-inch) squares kombu

6 dried shiitake mushrooms, or 6 slices dried porcini mushrooms

6 cloves garlic, peeled

2 (1-inch) pieces of fresh ginger

3 tablespoons Chinese five-spice powder

1 tablespoon whole black peppercorns

1 bunch cilantro

1 (16-ounce) package *phở* rice noodles, often sold as *bánh phở*

1 head broccoli, stemmed and separated into florets

2 large carrots, sliced on the diagonal

1 cup snow peas, trimmed

Salt and freshly ground black pepper

1 yellow onion, halved lengthwise and very thinly sliced

Lime wedges, for serving

Mung bean sprouts, for serving

Sliced jalapeño chiles, for serving

Fresh basil, for serving

Hoisin sauce, for serving (optional)

To make the broth, cook the onion rings over a direct flame (over a gas burner or on a preheated grill) until the bottom is blackened. Flip and cook until the other side is blackened. (Alternatively, the onions can be charred on a baking sheet under a preheated broiler.)

In a large pot, combine the blackened onions, water, Sriracha, liquid aminos, kombu, shiitakes, garlic, ginger, five-spice powder, and peppercorns. Tear a majority of

CONTINUED

the cilantro leaves from their stems. Set the leaves aside, and add the stems to the pot. Bring the broth to a boil, then immediately lower the heat, cover, and simmer gently for 2 hours. (Alternatively, cook in a slow cooker set on low heat for up to 8 hours.) Strain the broth through a fine-mesh sieve and discard the solids. Keep it warm or reheat gently just before serving.

To assemble the dish, fill a large bowl with warm water. Submerge the rice noodles and let soak for 20 minutes.

In a medium saucepan, bring ¹/₂ inch of water to a simmer over medium heat. Add the broccoli, carrots, and snow peas and season lightly with salt and pepper. Cover and cook until the vegetables are just tender, about 4 minutes. Drain well.

Drain the noodles and divide them among serving bowls. Top each serving with the cooked vegetables and sliced onion, then cover with the hot broth. Serve the lime wedges, bean sprouts, jalapeños, basil, hoisin sauce, and reserved cilantro leaves on a platter, letting diners personalize their bowls with the goodies they like. Instruct guests to tear the basil leaves into small pieces and squeeze the lime over their soup. By the time they're through, it will have been just enough time for the noodles to finish softening in the hot broth!

MOUTH ON FIRE MINESTRONE

Minestrone is a wonderful rustic Italian soup that doesn't really have a prescribed recipe because it was traditionally made with whatever vegetables were available, and made thicker and heartier with beans and pasta. I beg you to use this version, which couldn't be easier, as a starting point for your own imaginative creations based on whatever vegetables are fresh and in season at your market.
MAKES 4 TO 6 SERVINGS

4 cups vegetable stock

1/4 cup Sriracha

6 Roma tomatoes, diced

3 carrots, chopped

3 stalks celery, chopped

1 red onion, diced

1 large zucchini, halved lengthwise and chopped

3 cloves garlic, minced

2 bay leaves

1 tablespoon minced fresh oregano, or 1 1/2 teaspoons dried

1 3/4 cups cooked cannellini beans, or 1 (15-ounce) can, undrained

1 bunch kale, stemmed and chopped

Juice of 1 lemon

Salt and freshly ground black pepper

In a large Dutch oven or soup pot over medium-high heat, combine the stock, Sriracha, tomatoes, carrots, celery, onion, zucchini, garlic, bay leaves, and oregano. Bring to a boil, then immediately lower the heat, cover, and simmer for 15 minutes. Discard the bay leaves. Stir in the beans and kale and cook until both are tender, 5 to 7 minutes. Stir in the lemon juice, then season with salt and pepper to taste. Serve immediately. Stored in the refrigerator, leftovers will keep for 1 week.

SOON DUBU JJIGAE

Korea loves fermented chiles and garlic, and this Korean dish—*soon* (silken) *dubu* (tofu) *jjigae* (stew)—is, in my mind, the perfect convergence of spicy glory, incredible texture, and amazing flavor. It derives much of its character and soul (Seoul?) from a Korean chile paste called *gochujang*, available at Asian markets or online. I hope you'll do yourself the favor of tracking some down, but in a pinch, you can substitute more Sriracha. **MAKES 4 TO 6 SERVINGS**

4 cups water

3 (4-inch) squares kombu

1 tablespoon white or yellow miso

2 cups vegan kimchi, undrained

2 tablespoons toasted sesame oil or vegetable oil

1 large zucchini, quartered lengthwise and sliced

3 green onions, white and green parts, sliced on the diagonal

4 cloves garlic, minced

¹/₄ cup Sriracha

2 tablespoons *gochujang*

1 tablespoon Bragg Liquid Aminos or low-sodium soy sauce

2 (14-ounce) packages silken tofu, drained and cubed

1 (3- to 4-ounce) package enoki mushrooms (optional)

Combine the water, kombu, and miso in a saucepan over medium-high heat. Bring to a boil, then immediately lower the heat and simmer for 5 minutes. Remove from the heat and let sit for 10 minutes. Stir the broth until the miso is dissolved, then strain into a bowl and discard the kombu.

Meanwhile, drain the kimchi in a fine-mesh sieve set over a small bowl, pressing firmly to extract as much liquid as possible. Set the liquid aside and coarsely chop the kimchi.

Heat the oil in a large Dutch oven or soup pot over high heat. Add the zucchini and green onions and sauté until softened slightly, 3 to 5 minutes. Add the garlic and chopped kimchi and sauté just until the garlic is fragrant, about 30 seconds. Add the Sriracha, *gochujang*, liquid aminos, and reserved kimchi juice and stir to coat the vegetables evenly. Add the broth and tofu, stir gently, and bring to a vigorous boil for 2 minutes.

Trim away the bottom inch of the enoki mushrooms. Ladle the bubbling hot soup into bowls, top with the mushrooms, and serve immediately.

Ⓥ For a richer version, feel free to make this dish with the traditional addition of a raw egg that's broken into each serving at the table and stirred into the piping hot broth.

GF Commercial *gochujang* sometimes includes barley or wheat, so be sure to check the ingredients list. If you can't find a GF-friendly *gochujang*, simply replace it with more Sriracha.

SALADS
AND
SIDES

SRIRACHA BROCCOLI SLAW

I always strive to maintain some modicum of modesty in presenting my recipes, but I simply can't be shy about this one: it's ridiculously good. In fact, I'm willing to guess you'll start having strange broccoli cravings out of the blue shortly after trying it. **MAKES 4 TO 6 SERVINGS**

3 oranges

¹/₄ cup unsweetened dried cranberries or unsweetened dried cherries

¹/₂ cup vegan mayonnaise or Flax Mayonnaise (page 17)

2 tablespoons Bragg Liquid Aminos or low-sodium soy sauce

2 tablespoons Sriracha

2 large shallots, minced

2 tablespoons chopped fresh mint (optional)

1 tablespoon grated fresh ginger

1 (12-ounce) package broccoli slaw mix, or 6 ounces broccoli stems and 6 ounces carrot, grated

1 red bell pepper, julienned

¹/₄ cup raw sunflower seed kernels

Salt and freshly ground black pepper

Mince the zest of 1 orange and set aside. Juice all 3 oranges. In a small nonreactive bowl, combine the juice and dried cranberries and let sit at room temperature until the cranberries have plumped up and are slightly softened, about 2 hours. Drain, reserving ¹/₄ cup of the juice. (Drink the rest; it's damn good for you.)

In a small bowl, mix the vegan mayonnaise, liquid aminos, Sriracha, shallots, mint, ginger, and reserved orange juice. In a large bowl, toss together the broccoli slaw mix, cranberries, and bell pepper. Add the vegan mayo mixture and sunflower seed kernels and toss until evenly coated. Season with salt and pepper to taste. Cover and refrigerate for at least 30 minutes. Stored in the refrigerator, leftovers will keep for 3 days.

KICKED-UP CAPRESE

Caprese salad is awesome, and it's ridiculously easy to make. So much so that I'm surprised I don't see it served more often when people host get-togethers. For this vegan version, firm tofu is soaked in brine to mimic the texture and sweet saltiness of buffalo mozzarella. Of course, I've thrown in a little Sriracha for good measure. MAKES 4 TO 6 SERVINGS

3 cups warm water

$^1/_4$ cup kosher salt

$^1/_4$ cup Sriracha

2 cloves garlic, minced

2 tablespoons nutritional yeast flakes

1 tablespoon white or yellow miso (optional)

1 (14-ounce) package firm tofu, drained

2 large heirloom or beefsteak tomatoes, each cut into 8 slices

6 to 8 fresh basil leaves

Extra-virgin olive oil, for drizzling

Aged balsamic vinegar, for drizzling

Kosher salt or coarse sea salt and freshly ground black pepper

In a large measuring cup, combine the water, salt, Sriracha, garlic, nutritional yeast, and miso and stir until the salt has dissolved. Let cool to room temperature. Using a large chef's knife, split the tofu blocks in half horizontally, then cut each piece crosswise into quarters. Next, cut each piece diagonally to form 16 tofu triangles. Put the tofu into a gallon-size ziplock bag set inside a large bowl. Pour in the brine. Push out as much excess air as possible and seal the bag tightly. Make sure the tofu is completely submerged. Refrigerate for at least 2 hours or overnight.

Remove the tofu from the brine, discarding any excess liquid. On a large platter (or individual serving plates if you prefer), arrange the tomatoes and tofu, alternating them with each slice slightly overlapping the previous one.

Tear the basil leaves into small pieces by hand and sprinkle them over the salad. Drizzle a friendly amount of olive oil and balsamic vinegar over the top and around the plate. (More Sriracha is of course welcomed here, too.) Season with salt and pepper and serve immediately.

(V) Feel free to use 2 (8-ounce) balls of fresh buffalo mozzarella packed in brine in place of the tofu. Forgo the water, salt, nutritional yeast, and miso. Instead, simply drain the liquid from the cheese into a bowl. Mix with the Sriracha and garlic, then pour back into the containers, submerging the cheese. Refrigerate for 2 hours. Discard the soaking liquid, slice the cheese, and assemble the salad as directed.

SRIRACHA SALT You can use Sriracha salt to sprinkle over this dish, or to rim cocktail glasses, or on popcorn, French fries, edamame, baked potatoes, or, y'know . . . *anything!*

To make it, preheat the oven to 350°F and line a baking sheet with parchment paper. In a small bowl, mix $1/2$ cup kosher salt and 5 teaspoons Sriracha. Spread in a thin, even layer on the lined baking sheet. Put the baking sheet in the preheated oven and immediately turn off the heat. Let the salt sit in the residual heat until completely dry. The drying time can vary widely depending on many factors, but it usually ranges from 2 to 3 hours. Store in an airtight container.

EDAMAME-SRIRACHA SUCCOTASH

To chill or not to chill: that is the question. While it's true that succotash is delightful served warm, I've always enjoyed it served cold as a refreshing salad at summertime picnics. For me, it offers the brightest taste of the season, bursting with the crisp, sweet splendor of fresh, raw corn kernels. **MAKES 4 TO 6 SERVINGS**

2 tablespoons toasted sesame oil or extra-virgin olive oil

1 red onion, diced

1 red bell pepper, diced

3 cloves garlic, minced

2 cups fresh or frozen shelled edamame
Salt and freshly ground black pepper

2 cups fresh or frozen, thawed corn kernels

2 Roma tomatoes, diced

1/4 cup Sriracha

1/4 cup chopped fresh cilantro or parsley, plus more sprigs for garnish

2 tablespoons apple cider vinegar or freshly squeezed lime juice

1 tablespoon Bragg liquid aminos or low-sodium soy sauce

Heat 1 tablespoon of the oil in a cast-iron or nonstick skillet over medium heat. Add the onion and bell pepper and sauté until softened, 5 to 7 minutes. Add the garlic and sauté just until fragrant, about 30 seconds. Let cool to room temperature.

In a medium saucepan, bring 1/2 inch of water to a simmer over medium heat. Add the edamame and season lightly with salt and pepper. Cover and cook until just tender and heated through, about 4 minutes. Drain well and let cool to room temperature. (If using frozen edamame, cook on the stove top according to the package directions; don't microwave.) Transfer to a bowl.

Add the onion mixture, corn, tomatoes, Sriracha, cilantro, vinegar, liquid aminos, and remaining tablespoon of oil and mix well. Season with salt and pepper to taste. Cover and refrigerate for at least 30 minutes. Taste just before serving and add more vinegar or Sriracha if desired. Serve garnished with cilantro sprigs. Stored in the refrigerator, leftovers will keep for 3 days.

WARM DIJON-SRIRACHA POTATO SALAD WITH TOASTED HAZELNUTS

There's a great chain of restaurants in the Los Angeles area called Lemonade. They come up with insane flavor combinations that most people wouldn't think of in a bajillion years. On my first trip there, I tried a cold beet salad made with pickled onions and a hazelnut vinaigrette that knocked my socks off. It's been on my mind ever since, and I used it as a loose inspiration for this mighty tasty dish. **MAKES 4 TO 6 SERVINGS**

¹/₄ cup hazelnuts

2 pounds small Yukon gold or russet potatoes, scrubbed

Salt

1 large red onion, halved lengthwise and thinly sliced

2 stalks celery, diced

¹/₄ cup chopped fresh flat-leaf parsley, plus more for garnish

¹/₄ cup chopped fresh dill

2 cloves garlic, minced

¹/₄ cup apple cider vinegar

¹/₄ cup Dijon mustard

3 tablespoons Sriracha

2 tablespoons extra-virgin olive oil

Freshly ground black pepper

Preheat the oven to 350°F.

Spread the hazelnuts in a single layer on a rimmed baking sheet and bake for about 10 minutes, until golden and fragrant. (Keep an eye on them, as they can go from delightfully toasty to burnt in a matter of seconds.) Carefully transfer to a clean kitchen towel, wrap the towel around them, and let sit for 1 minute to steam from the residual heat. Rub the hazelnuts together inside the towel to loosen and remove a majority of the skins. Transfer the skinned hazelnuts to a large bowl.

Cut the potatoes in half lengthwise, then cut each piece in half crosswise. Put the potatoes in a large saucepan, add water to cover, and season with a generous amount of salt. Bring to a boil over high heat, then immediately lower the heat, cover, and simmer until the potatoes are fork-tender, about 10 minutes. Drain well.

Add the onion, celery, parsley, dill, garlic, vinegar, mustard, Sriracha, and olive oil to the hazelnuts and mix well. Add the potatoes and toss with a rubber spatula until evenly coated. Season with salt and pepper to taste. Serve immediately, garnished with parsley.

V A mighty fine bonus touch would be 2 grated hard-boiled eggs, added along with the potatoes.

GF Choose a Dijon mustard that doesn't contain distilled white vinegar, which is usually derived from grain. Ideally, it should be made with white wine, wine vinegar, or verjuice.

TOASTING NUTS AND SEEDS

Toasting nuts and seeds is super simple. With hazelnuts, toasting helps loosen their papery skin; with other goodies (like pine nuts, sesame seeds, almonds, etc.), toasting intensifies flavor and makes for a tastier end product.

To toast almonds, cashews, and other nuts, spread the nuts in a single layer on a rimmed baking sheet and bake for about 10 minutes, until golden and fragrant.

To toast pine nuts and seeds, place them in a dry skillet over medium-high heat and cook, stirring or shaking the pan frequently to toast evenly. Cook until the nuts or seeds darken slightly and become aromatic.

Whatever you do, don't leave their side! The line between toasted and burned is a fine one and takes mere seconds to cross.

STIR-FRIED ASPARAGUS AND GREEN BEAN SALAD WITH DYN-O-MITE DRESSING

This thick, creamy dressing is a real workhorse and can stand up to the most robust of salads . . . like this one! The green beans and asparagus add some serious heft, making this hearty salad a perfect entrée choice for even the largest of appetites. **MAKES 4 TO 6 SERVINGS**

Dressing

- $1/2$ cup raw whole cashews, soaked in water for 2 hours
- 1 red bell pepper, quartered
- 3 tablespoons Sriracha
- 2 tablespoons freshly squeezed lemon juice
- 2 cloves garlic, peeled
- Salt and freshly ground black pepper

Salad

- 2 large handfuls fresh green beans, trimmed and cut into 2-inch lengths
- 1 bunch asparagus, trimmed and cut into 2-inch lengths
- 10 ounces mixed salad greens
- 1 small red onion, halved lengthwise and thinly sliced
- 1 carrot, grated
- 2 tablespoons raw sunflower seed kernels (optional)
- 2 tablespoons extra-virgin olive oil
- 1 clove garlic, minced
- Salt and freshly ground black pepper

To make the dressing, drain the cashews. Put them in a food processor or high-speed blender and add the bell pepper, Sriracha, lemon juice, and garlic. Process until very smooth, pausing once or twice to scrape down the sides with a rubber spatula. Season with salt and pepper to taste. Transfer to an airtight container and let sit for at least 30 minutes. (The dressing can be kept at room temperature for 4 hours or be stored in the refrigerator for up to 1 week. If refrigerating, take it out 30 minutes before serving to let it come to room temperature.)

To make the salad, fill a large bowl with ice water. In a medium saucepan, bring $1/2$ inch of water to a simmer over medium heat. Add the green beans, cover, and cook for 3 minutes. Add the asparagus, cover, and cook just until tender, about 5 minutes. Drain through a colander and immediately dunk the colander into the prepared ice bath to halt the cooking and preserve the bright green color of the veggies. Let cool for several minutes, then lift the colander out of the ice water. Drain well, then spread the veggies on a clean kitchen towel or paper towels. Cover with an additional towel or more paper towels and pat dry.

In a large bowl, toss together the salad greens, onion, carrot, and sunflower seeds. Drizzle the dressing over the salad, adding it to taste, and toss again. Divide the salad among serving bowls.

Heat the oil in a cast-iron or nonstick skillet over high heat. Add the garlic and sauté just until fragrant, about 30 seconds. Add the asparagus and green beans and stir-fry just until they pick up a little shine and color, about 4 minutes. Season with salt and pepper to taste. Top each salad with the stir-fried veggies. Serve immediately.

MASSAGED RAW KALE The Dyn-O-Mite Dressing is quite versatile, and I really enjoy it over massaged kale. Though not nearly as kinky as it sounds, massaged kale is just as good as it is good for you!

To make massaged kale, simply stem and chop one head of kale and place it in a bowl, mix in the juice of 1 lemon, a splash of olive oil, and a touch of salt and pepper. Using your hands, rub and squeeze the kale really firmly (don't be shy about it) to help break down the tough fibers. Once it's softened up, let sit for 10 minutes, rub once more, and toss with your favorite dressing . . . aka this one!

GRILLED SHISHITO PEPPERS WITH SRIRACHA SATAY SAUCE

Shishito peppers whisper the subtlest bit of heat but pack a humongous amount of flavor, *especially* when grilled to smoky perfection. If you can't find them at your local Asian market, you can substitute Spanish Padrón peppers or Anaheim chiles. The refreshing satay sauce in this recipe can be used with plenty of other dishes, such as grilled tofu skewers, or as the perfect dipping sauce for spring rolls. Coarse sea salt isn't essential for seasoning the peppers, but I highly recommend it; you'll love the pop of the bigger crystals on these bad boys. You can also use Sriracha Salt (page 49) for extra kick.

MAKES 4 TO 6 SERVINGS

Sriracha Satay Sauce

- 1 (14-ounce) can coconut milk
- 1/2 cup natural crunchy peanut butter, stirred well
- 1/3 cup Sriracha
- 1/2 small red onion, minced
- 1 clove garlic, minced
- 1 tablespoon Bragg Liquid Aminos or low-sodium soy sauce
- 2 teaspoons brown sugar

Grilled Peppers

- 3/4 pound shishito peppers
- 2 tablespoons extra-virgin olive oil
  Shichimi tōgarashi, for serving (optional; see sidebar, page 58)
  Coarse sea salt and freshly ground black pepper
- 2 tablespoons chopped fresh cilantro, for garnish

To make the sauce, combine the coconut milk, peanut butter, Sriracha, onion, garlic, liquid aminos, and sugar in a medium saucepan over medium heat. Bring to a simmer and stir to incorporate the peanut butter. Lower the heat and simmer, stirring occasionally, until slightly thickened, about 5 minutes. Remove from the heat, transfer to an airtight container, and refrigerate for at least 1 hour.

To prepare the peppers, preheat a grill, grill pan, or broiler to high heat. In a large bowl, toss the peppers with the oil until evenly coated. Spread the peppers in a single layer on the grill or a broiler pan. Cook until the skin is lightly charred and blistered,

CONTINUED

about 7 minutes total, flipping once about halfway through.

Serve immediately, sprinkled with *shichimi tōgarashi*, salt, and black pepper to taste. Garnish with the cilantro and serve the sauce alongside in bowls for dipping.

SHICHIMI TŌGARASHI My good friend Linzy May Mahoney, publisher of the glorious Los Angeles–based *Edible Westside* magazine, introduced me to *shichimi*, a Japanese blend of seven seasonings that is downright addictive. It incorporates roasted orange peel, black sesame seeds, white sesame seeds, chile flakes, ginger, *sanshō* (a Japanese pepper similar to Szechuan pepper), and nori. A light sprinkling on finished dishes adds an incredible amount of flavor that will send your taste buds soaring. It can be found in most Asian markets or online.

SPICY TABBOULEH-STUFFED DOLMAS

I never appreciated the true power of parsley until my first glorious taste of flavorful flat-leaf parsley in a batch of tabbouleh. My love for tabbouleh has grown more and more since that day, as has my affinity for stuffed grape leaves (aka dolmas). One day, a candle flickered in my brain and I thought to combine the two. The result is a Mediterranean fantasy come true. MAKES 6 TO 8 SERVINGS

1 cup bulgur wheat or quinoa

1/4 cup golden raisins

2 cups boiling water

3 lemons

1 cup chopped fresh flat-leaf parsley

3 Roma tomatoes, diced

1 bunch green onions, white and green parts, diced

1 large carrot, grated

1 Persian cucumber, or 1/2 English cucumber, diced

2 cloves garlic, minced

1/4 cup Sriracha

2 tablespoons Bragg Liquid Aminos or low-sodium soy sauce

2 tablespoons extra-virgin olive oil, plus more for brushing

Salt and freshly ground black pepper

24 to 30 grape leaves packed in brine

In a large heatproof bowl, combine the bulgur and raisins, then pour in the boiling water. Cover and let sit until the water is absorbed and the grains are tender, about 10 minutes. (If using quinoa, let sit for about 30 minutes.)

Mince the zest of 1 lemon, then juice all 3 lemons. In a large bowl, mix the parsley, tomatoes, green onions, carrot, cucumber, garlic, Sriracha, liquid aminos, oil, zest, and juice. Add the bulgur and toss until well combined. (For a side dish of tabbouleh, stop here, chill completely, then season with salt and pepper to taste before serving.)

Rinse the grape leaves under cool running water to reduce their saltiness. Lay them out flat on a work service with the veins facing up. Trim away the stems. Put about 1 tablespoon of the tabbouleh in the center of each grape leaf. Roll each leaf up tightly around the filling like a mini burrito, tucking in the sides. Stack them on a serving plate or in a container seam side down, cover with a damp paper towel, and chill for at least 1 hour before serving. (They will be even better after a day or two, in my opinion.) Brush with a bit of olive oil just before serving so they're nice and shiny. Stored in the refrigerator, leftovers will keep for 1 week.

BREAKFAST
OF
CHAMPIONS

SRIRACHA AND GREEN ONION BISCUITS WITH COUNTRY MUSHROOM GRAVY

Not that we veggie lovers have anything to prove to die-hard carnivores, but this is one dish I like to put out there quietly, simply describing it as "biscuits and gravy." It's amazing how quickly it gets devoured by folks of all persuasions, with nary a thought that it might be . . . *gasp* . . . vegan! If you work quickly enough when making the gravy, it will be ready just as the biscuits come out of the oven or shortly thereafter. If you prefer a more leisurely pace, make the gravy first, then gently reheat it before serving.
MAKES 4 TO 6 SERVINGS

Biscuits

- 1 cup all-purpose flour
- 2 teaspoons baking powder
- $^1/_4$ teaspoon baking soda
- $^1/_2$ teaspoon fine sea salt
- $^1/_4$ cup cold nonhydrogenated vegetable shortening (such as Earth Balance) or vegan butter (see note, page 12), cubed
- $^1/_2$ cup unsweetened nondairy milk
- 3 tablespoons Sriracha
- 4 green onions, green part only, sliced on the diagonal

Gravy

- 2 tablespoons extra-virgin olive oil
- 8 ounces cremini or button mushrooms, minced
- 2 large shallots, minced
  Salt and freshly ground black pepper
- 2 cloves garlic, minced
- 1 tablespoon chopped fresh rosemary
- 2 tablespoons cornstarch, or $^1/_4$ cup all-purpose flour
- 2 cups vegetable stock
- 2 tablespoons apple cider vinegar
- 1 tablespoon nutritional yeast flakes (optional)

- 2 green onions, green part only, sliced on the diagonal, for garnish

To make the biscuits, preheat the oven to 400°F. Line a baking sheet with parchment paper.

In a bowl, mix the flour, baking powder, baking soda, and salt. Add the shortening and cut it in using a pastry blender or a fork. Once the shortening has more or less coated every fleck of flour, small pea-size balls of dough should begin to form. At that point, switch to a wooden spoon and stir in the nondairy milk, Sriracha, and green onions, taking care not to overwork the dough. Once it has formed a shaggy mass, stop mixing.

On a lightly floured workspace, press the dough into a rectangle, about 1½ to 2 inches thick. Cut out 6 large rounds and space them evenly on the lined baking sheet. Bake for 15 to 20 minutes, until light golden brown.

Meanwhile, make the gravy. Heat the oil in a cast-iron or nonstick skillet over high heat. Add the mushrooms and shallots, season lightly with salt and pepper, and sauté until the mushrooms have given off their moisture and are slightly browned, about

5 minutes. Add the garlic and rosemary and sauté just until the garlic is fragrant, about 30 seconds. Stir in the cornstarch, coating the mushroom mixture evenly. Immediately add 1 cup of the stock, stirring to avoid lumps and scraping up any brown bits that may be stuck to the skillet. Stir in the remaining stock, the vinegar, and the nutritional yeast and bring to a boil. Lower the heat and simmer, stirring often, until thickened, with no lingering chalky raw cornstarch taste, 10 to 15 minutes. Season with salt and pepper to taste.

Split the biscuits in half horizontally. Serve with their insides facing up, drowned in a flood of gravy and garnished with the green onions and plenty of pepper.

GF For the biscuits, use your favorite gluten-free flour or baking mix. (If the baking mix already contains salt, baking powder, or baking soda, omit those ingredients when mixing the biscuits.) For the gravy, cornstarch is gluten-free. If you prefer to use flour, make sure it's gluten-free.

LIGHT MY FIRE POTATO-PARSNIP LATKES

So there are these vegetarian bloggers—Alex Brown and Evan George—who run one heck of a site called Hot Knives. Beyond being endlessly clever and entertaining, they've also spawned an awesome cookbook: *The Hot Knives Vegetarian Cookbook: Salad Daze*. It has a recipe for Kohlrabi Latkes that absolutely blew my mind—and got me thinking about more root veggie possibilities for latkes. Armed with that inspiration, ladies and gentlemen, I give you the parsnip-potato latke! **MAKES 4 TO 6 SERVINGS**

3 large parsnips

2 tablespoons extra-virgin olive oil, plus more for frying

2 large russet potatoes

1 bunch green onions, green part only, sliced on the diagonal

$1/4$ cup chopped fresh flat-leaf parsley

3 cloves garlic, minced

$1/4$ cup Sriracha

Salt and freshly ground black pepper

Cilantro-Coconut Crema (page 34) or vegan sour cream, for serving (optional)

Applesauce, for serving (optional)

In a medium saucepan, bring $1/2$ inch of water to a simmer over medium heat. Dice 2 of the parsnips and put them in the pan. Cover and cook until fork-tender, about 5 minutes. Drain well, then pat dry with a clean kitchen towel or paper towels. Transfer to a food processor or high-speed blender. With the processor running, slowly add the olive oil, processing until smooth and pausing once or twice to scrape down the sides with a rubber spatula.

Preheat the oven to 200°F. Put a wire rack atop a baking sheet or line a baking sheet with foil. Put the baking sheet in the oven.

Working quickly to help prevent browning, peel and grate the potatoes along with the remaining parsnip. Firmly squeeze the grated veggies in your hands over a colander set in the sink or a bowl to expel excess moisture. Transfer to a bowl, add the parsnip puree, green onions, parsley, garlic, and Sriracha and mix well. Season generously with salt and pepper.

Pour $1/4$ inch of olive oil into a large cast-iron or nonstick skillet. Heat over medium-high heat until the oil begins to shimmer and a tiny test fleck of the potato mixture sizzles immediately. (If it doesn't sizzle right away, the oil isn't hot enough and the latkes will absorb a lot more oil, making them more soggy than crisp. *No bueno.*) Form several patties by hand, using about $1/4$ cup of the mixture for each and flattening until about $1/2$ inch thick. Carefully place them in the hot oil and fry until the bottom is crispy and dark brown, about 4 minutes. Flip and cook until the other side is dark brown, 3 to 4 minutes. Transfer to the wire rack in the oven to keep warm. Once all of the latkes are cooked, serve immediately, garnishing each plate with big dollops of crema and applesauce.

Ⓥ Feel free to prepare the vegetarian version of Cilantro-Coconut Crema (page 34), or substitute plain sour cream or crème fraîche for the crema.

MEAN QUICHE FLORENTINE

I've made vegan quiches with tofu in the filling, and they tasted great, but I always wanted more from the texture. Then I found my answer, thanks to Isa Chandra Moskowitz's splendiferous book *Vegan Brunch: Homestyle Recipes Worth Waking Up For*. The secret? Cashews. **MAKES 6 TO 8 SERVINGS**

Crust

- 1¹/₂ cups all-purpose flour, chilled in the freezer for 30 minutes, plus more for dusting
- ¹/₂ teaspoon baking powder
  Pinch of salt
- ³/₄ cup cold nonhydrogenated vegetable shortening (such as Earth Balance) or vegan butter (see page 12), cubed
- ¹/₂ teaspoon apple cider vinegar (optional)
- 2 to 6 tablespoons ice water

Filling

- 2 tablespoons extra-virgin olive oil
- 1 red onion, halved lengthwise and thinly sliced
- 2 cloves garlic, minced
- 1 large bunch spinach, stemmed, or 1 (10-ounce) package frozen spinach, thawed and drained
- ¹/₂ cup raw whole cashews, soaked in water for 2 hours
- 2 (14-ounce) packages extra-firm tofu, drained and crumbled
- ¹/₄ cup Sriracha
- ¹/₄ cup nutritional yeast flakes
- ¹/₂ teaspoon ground turmeric
- ¹/₄ teaspoon ground nutmeg (optional)
  Salt and freshly ground black pepper

To make the crust, combine the flour, baking powder, and salt in a large bowl. Add the shortening and cut it in using a pastry blender or a fork. Once the shortening has more or less coated every fleck of flour, small pea-size balls of dough should begin to form. At that point, switch to a wooden spoon and stir in the vinegar and 2 tablespoons of the ice water. Mix in more water, 1 tablespoon at a time, until the dough comes together into a solid mass. Once the wooden spoon gets unwieldy, mix the dough with clean hands, taking care not to overwork it. Roll the dough into a ball, then flatten into a round disk. Wrap in plastic wrap and refrigerate for 30 minutes.

Preheat the oven to 400°F.

To make the filling, heat the oil in a cast-iron or nonstick skillet over medium heat. Add the onion and sauté until softened, 5 to 7 minutes. Add the garlic and sauté just until fragrant, about 30 seconds. Add the spinach and sauté until completely wilted and its moisture has evaporated, about 5 minutes. Remove from the heat.

Drain the cashews and pulse them in a food processor until finely chopped. Add the tofu, Sriracha, nutritional yeast, turmeric, and nutmeg and process until well blended and mostly smooth. Transfer to a large bowl, add the spinach mixture, and mix well. Season with salt and pepper to taste.

To assemble and bake the quiche, lightly dust a work surface with flour and roll out the dough into a 12-inch circle. Transfer to a 9-inch pie tin, trimming excess dough from the edges. Prick the dough all over with a fork. Bake for 10 minutes (this will parbake the crust).

Remove from the oven and fill with the tofu mixture, spreading it in an even layer and smoothing the top. Bake for 30 to 35 minutes, until the edges of the crust begin to brown. Let cool for at least 15 minutes before serving warm or at room temperature. Stored in the refrigerator, leftovers will keep for 3 days.

V When making the filling, feel free to use 2 cups half-and-half, $1^{1}/_{2}$ cup shredded Swiss cheese, and 4 eggs in place of the cashews, tofu, nutritional yeast, and turmeric. In a medium bowl, beat the eggs, then add the half-and-half, cheese, Sriracha, and nutmeg and mix well. Season with salt and pepper and transfer to the parbaked crust. Bake as directed.

GF For the crust, use your favorite gluten-free flour or baking mix. (If the baking mix already contains salt or baking powder, omit those ingredients when mixing the dough.)

CALIFORNIA BENEDICT WITH SRIRACHA-CHIVE HOLLANDAISE

One of my favorite dishes from "my former life" was California Benedict, stacked high with spinach, tomato, and yummy, yummy avocado. I thought I'd have to say good-bye to it forever when I adopted a more vegan lifestyle, but Isa Chandra Moskowitz's incredible tome *Vegan Brunch: Homestyle Recipes Worth Waking Up For* thankfully proved me wrong. Her "Tofu Benny" showed me the light and served as a major inspiration, smoked salt and all, for this glorious Sriracha-spiked rendition! **MAKES 4 SERVINGS**

Brined Tofu

- 1 cup vegetable stock
- 2 tablespoons apple cider vinegar
- 1 tablespoon Bragg Liquid Aminos or low-sodium soy sauce
- 1 teaspoon smoked salt
- 1 (14-ounce) package firm tofu, drained

Sriracha-Chive Hollandaise Sauce

- 3/4 cup unsweetened almond milk
- 3 tablespoons Sriracha
- 1 tablespoon cornstarch
- 1/8 teaspoon ground turmeric
- 1 tablespoon extra-virgin olive oil
- 2 tablespoons minced fresh chives
- 2 tablespoons apple cider vinegar
- 1 1/2 tablespoons nutritional yeast flakes
- 1 tablespoon freshly squeezed lemon juice
- 1 teaspoon white or yellow miso (optional)

- 2 tablespoons extra-virgin olive oil
- 2 English muffins

- 1 cup lightly packed spinach or arugula leaves, for serving
- 1 heirloom or beefsteak tomato (about the width of an English muffin), ends removed and cut into 4 thick slices
- 1 large, ripe Hass avocado, for garnish
  Minced fresh chives, for garnish
  Smoked salt and freshly ground black pepper

To prepare the tofu, in a large measuring cup, combine the stock, vinegar, liquid aminos, and smoked salt and stir until the salt has dissolved. Using a large chef's knife, split the tofu in half horizontally, then cut each piece crosswise into quarters. Put the tofu in a gallon-size ziplock bag set aside in a large bowl and pour in the marinade. Push out as much excess air as possible and seal the bag tightly. Make sure the tofu is

CONTINUED

completely submerged. Marinate in the refrigerator for at least 1 hour or overnight.

To make the sauce, combine the almond milk, Sriracha, cornstarch, and turmeric in a small bowl and whisk until smooth and well combined. Heat the oil in a saucepan over medium heat. Add the chives and sauté just until fragrant, about 30 seconds. Stir in the vinegar and cook for 30 seconds. Pour in the almond milk mixture and bring to a simmer. Lower the heat and simmer until thickened, about 7 minutes, whisking frequently to avoid lumps. Stir in the nutritional yeast, lemon juice, and miso. Let cool while the tofu cooks. If it cools too much, reheat gently on the stove.

To cook the tofu and assemble the dish, remove the tofu from its marinade, discarding any excess liquid. Pat dry with paper towels. Heat the 2 tablespoons of oil in a cast-iron or nonstick skillet over medium heat. Add the tofu and cook until browned on both sides, about 15 minutes total.

In the last 5 minutes of cooking time, split and toast the English muffins. Put a muffin half on each plate, nooks and crannies facing up. Put a small handful of spinach leaves on each, followed by a slice of tomato,

two pieces of the tofu, and a glorious smothering of warm sauce. (Don't drown it though, as you want everyone to see the layers and appreciate the beauty.) Garnish with fanned slices of the avocado, a sprinkling of chives, a pinch of smoked salt, and freshly ground pepper. Serve immediately.

V Feel free to substitute the traditional poached egg for the tofu in this dish or, if you like, use both! (The tofu is genuinely delicious with the other ingredients in this dish.) As for the sauce, you can add Sriracha and chives to your favorite hollandaise sauce recipe, but this recipe is actually much easier than traditional hollandaise. Plus, it isn't 90 percent butter, so it's healthier while still tasting damn good.

GF Use gluten-free English muffins, hamburger buns, or any type of gluten-free bread. (If you use bread and want circular pieces, cut them out with a large round cookie cutter.)

> **OVER THE TOP TIP** For a truly gourmet rendition (with more Sriracha!), use potato-parsnip latkes (page 64) in place of the English muffins.

SRIRACHA SHAKSHUKA

Shakshuka is the most incredible breakfast fare that you've likely never heard of. Popular in Northern Africa and Israel, it's a dish of eggs poached in a spicy tomato sauce (see photo, page 60). I admittedly had it only once before researching and developing this vegan version, but I remember that first bite so vividly. Unfortunately, the restaurant where I had it closed down, and I've been pining for it ever since. Serve this beautiful breakfast with some crusty bread to mop up all the ridiculously tasty sauce. **MAKES 4 TO 6 SERVINGS**

3 tablespoons extra-virgin olive oil

1 large red onion, thinly sliced

2 green bell peppers, cut into thin strips

4 cloves garlic, minced

1 tablespoon ground cumin

1 teaspoon smoked paprika

3 sprigs thyme

1 bay leaf

1 (28-ounce) can crushed tomatoes, undrained

$^1/_2$ cup water

$^1/_3$ cup Sriracha

Salt and freshly ground black pepper

8 ounces soft tofu, drained and cubed

2 tablespoons chopped fresh flat-leaf parsley, for garnish

Hearty rustic bread, for serving

Heat 2 tablespoons of the oil in a cast-iron or nonstick skillet over medium-high heat. Add the onion and sauté until softened, 5 to 7 minutes. Add the bell peppers and sauté for 5 minutes. Add the garlic, cumin, paprika, thyme, and bay leaf and sauté just until the garlic is fragrant, about 30 seconds. Add the tomatoes and their liquid, using a wooden spoon to scrape up any brown bits that may be stuck to the skillet. Stir in the water and Sriracha. Bring to a boil, then immediately lower the heat and simmer gently for 10 minutes.

Discard the thyme sprigs and bay leaf if you can find them easily. Season with salt

CONTINUED

and pepper to taste. Make 4 to 6 divots in the mixture, depending on the number of portions you intend to serve. Divide the tofu evenly among the divots. Sprinkle a pinch of salt and pepper over the tofu in each divot. Cover and simmer until the tofu is heated through, 8 to 10 minutes. Remove from the heat. Drizzle the remaining tablespoon of olive oil over the top, garnish with the parsley, and serve immediately.

V Feel free to substitute 4 to 6 free-range eggs in place of the tofu, cracking one into each divot and taking care not to break the yolks. Cover and cook until the whites are set but the yolks are still slightly runny, about 8 to 10 minutes.

BÁNH XÈO

My good friend Phi Nguyen's family was instrumental in shaping my love of food and cooking. Heck, his house is where I had my first fateful taste of the almighty rooster sauce. His mom and sister are rock stars in the kitchen, and their cooking has left a massive, indelible mark on my life. *Bánh xèo* (loosely pronounced "bahn say-oh") is a breakfast dish similar to a savory crêpe filled with all sorts of tasty Vietnamese treats. The turmeric that's traditionally used gives the crêpe an omelet-like yellow hue, but with the addition of Sriracha, it becomes a beautiful, fiery orange that will surely get your taste buds excited about the adventure they're about to embark on. **MAKES 4 TO 6 SERVINGS**

Crêpes

- 1¹/₂ cups rice flour (not sweet rice flour)
- ¹/₂ teaspoon ground turmeric
- ¹/₂ teaspoon fine sea salt
- 1 cup coconut milk
- ¹/₄ cup Sriracha
- ¹/₄ to ¹/₂ cup water
- 1 tablespoon extra-virgin olive oil
- 2 green onions, green and white parts, sliced on the diagonal

Filling

- 1 cup vegetable stock
- 2 tablespoons apple cider vinegar
- 1 tablespoon Bragg Liquid Aminos or low-sodium soy sauce
- 1 (14-ounce) package firm tofu, drained and cubed
- 2 tablespoons extra-virgin olive oil
- 4 ounces shiitake, cremini, or button mushrooms, sliced
- 4 green onions, green and white parts, sliced on the diagonal
- 3 cloves garlic, minced
  Salt and freshly ground black pepper

- 2 cups fresh mung bean sprouts
  Large leaves of Romaine lettuce, for serving
  Fresh Thai basil sprigs, for serving
  Fresh cilantro sprigs, for serving
  Vegan *nước chấm* sauce (see sidebar, page 77), for dipping

To make the crêpes, mix the rice flour, turmeric, and salt in a small bowl. Add the coconut milk and whisk until smooth. Whisk in the Sriracha and ¹/₄ cup water. Add more water if needed to achieve a consistency that's a bit thinner than pancake batter—liquid but not watery. Stir in the oil

CONTINUED

and green onions and set aside while you prepare the filling. (The batter can be made up to 2 days in advance and kept in the refrigerator.)

To make the filling, combine the stock, vinegar, and liquid aminos in a large measuring cup. Put the cubed tofu in a gallon-size ziplock bag set inside a large bowl and pour in the marinade. Push out as much excess air as possible and seal the bag tightly. Marinate in the refrigerator for at least 1 hour or overnight.

Remove the tofu from its marinade, reserving $1/4$ cup of the marinade and discarding the rest. Pat the tofu dry with paper towels.

Heat the oil in a large cast-iron or nonstick skillet over medium-high heat. Add the tofu and mushrooms, and sauté, turning the tofu gently, until the mushrooms have given off their moisture and are slightly browned, 5 to 7 minutes. Add the green onions and sauté for 1 minute. Add the garlic and sauté just until fragrant, about 30 seconds. Pour in the reserved marinade to deglaze the pan,

using a wooden spoon to scrape up all the stubborn, tasty brown bits. Cook, stirring occasionally, until the liquid has evaporated, about 2 to 3 minutes. Remove from the heat and season with salt and pepper to taste.

To bring it all together, preheat the oven to 200°F. Put a wire rack atop a baking sheet or line a baking sheet with foil. Put the baking sheet in the oven.

Heat a large nonstick skillet over medium heat. With a ladle, stir the batter, then spoon $1/3$ to $1/2$ cup of batter into the pan, tilting and swirling the pan to make sure the batter is evenly distributed. Spoon $1/4$ to $1/2$ cup of the vegetable mixture in an even layer on one half of the crêpe, leaving a border around the edges so the filling doesn't escape when the crêpe is folded over. Cook until the edges of the crêpe begin to dry and curl slightly, about 3 minutes. Add a generous handful of mung bean sprouts atop the vegetables and fold the other half of the crêpe over the filling. Cover and cook for 2 minutes. Transfer the finished crêpe to the wire rack in the oven to keep warm.

Once all of the crêpes are cooked, serve immediately, with communal plates of lettuce leaves, basil, and cilantro and individual bowls of nước chấm alongside. Traditionally, diners cut off large pieces of their *bánh xèo*, wrap each bite in a lettuce leaf with some basil and cilantro leaves, dip it into nước chấm, and devour it happily.

VEGAN NƯỚC CHẤM SAUCE

Nước chấm (loosely pronounced "nuke chum") is the traditional dipping sauce for Vietnamese spring rolls, and its sweet, umami-rich flavor works beautifully with these lettuce cups. It certainly isn't necessary, but if you've got a few extra minutes, I say go for it! **MAKES ABOUT 1 CUP**

$^1/_2$ cup warm water

$^1/_4$ cup sugar

$^1/_4$ cup Bragg Liquid Aminos or low-sodium soy sauce

3 tablespoons freshly squeezed lime juice

3 tablespoons rice vinegar (not the seasoned variety)

5 cloves garlic, minced

2 Thai chiles, minced

In a bowl, mix all the ingredients. Let sit for at least 1 hour. If serving the same day, cover and keep at room temperature. For longer storage, refrigerate for up to 2 weeks.

MAIN
DISHES

SRIRACHA-CAULIFLOWER MAC 'N' CHEEZE

Y'know, I was going to write this recipe using pasta, but then I got to thinkin' about how I made this book for people who love *veggies*. So I swapped cauliflower for the pasta, and it turned out *great!* For those who simply want pasta and will kill anyone who gets in their way, feel free to use 8 ounces of elbow macaroni, cooked until al dente, in place of the cauliflower. **MAKES 4 TO 6 SERVINGS**

Topping

- 2 tablespoons coconut oil or extra-virgin olive oil
- 1 cup panko bread crumbs

Cheeze Sauce

- $3/4$ cup raw whole cashews, soaked in water for 2 hours
- $1/4$ cup raw sunflower seed kernels
- $3/4$ cup nutritional yeast flakes
- $1^1/2$ teaspoons kosher salt
- 1 teaspoon dry mustard
- $1/2$ teaspoon freshly ground black pepper
- $1/2$ teaspoon ground nutmeg
- 2 tablespoons coconut oil or extra-virgin olive oil
- $1/2$ small sweet onion, diced
- $1/4$ cup all-purpose flour
- 2 cups unsweetened nondairy milk
- 3 tablespoons cornstarch
- $1/4$ cup Sriracha

- 1 large head cauliflower, cut into small florets
- Chopped fresh flat-leaf parsley, for garnish

To make the topping, melt the coconut oil in a large saucepan over medium heat. Gently stir in the panko, then turn off the heat and let the bread crumbs absorb the oil.

Preheat the oven to 400°F. Lightly spritz a 2-quart casserole dish with nonstick cooking spray.

To make the sauce, drain the cashews and pulse them in a food processor with the sunflower seeds until finely ground. Add the nutritional yeast, salt, mustard, pepper, and nutmeg and pulse until well combined.

Heat the coconut oil in a large saucepan over medium heat. Add the onion and sauté until softened, 5 to 7 minutes. Whisk in the flour. Cook for 2 to 3 minutes, stirring constantly to avoid lumps. In a small cup or bowl, whisk together $1/2$ cup of the nondairy milk and the cornstarch. Add to the pan, stirring constantly. Cook, still stirring constantly, until the mixture has thickened, then whisk in the remaining

1½ cups nondairy milk. Stir in the cashew mixture and Sriracha. Bring to a simmer, then immediately lower the heat and cook, stirring occasionally, until thickened and creamy, about 5 minutes. Season with salt and pepper to taste. Remove from the heat and cover to keep warm.

To assemble the dish, put ½ inch of water in a saucepan and bring to a simmer over medium heat. Add the cauliflower and season lightly with salt and pepper. Cover and cook until just tender, 4 to 6 minutes. Drain well, then pat dry with a clean kitchen towel or paper towels. Transfer to the prepared casserole dish. Pour the sauce over the cauliflower and top with the panko.

Bake for 15 to 20 minutes, until the topping is golden brown and the sauce is bubbling. Remove from the oven and let sit for 5 minutes so the molten cheeze lava can cool just a touch. Portion, plate, and serve garnished with parsley.

V To make a classic cheese sauce, heat 2 tablespoons butter or oil in a large saucepan. Add ½ sweet onion, diced, and sauté until softened, then stir in ¼ cup flour as directed. Whisk in ½ cup whole milk. Once the milk has thickened slightly, stir in another 1½ cups whole milk, then 1 cup heavy cream, 1 teaspoon kosher salt, ½ teaspoon freshly ground black pepper, and ½ teaspoon ground nutmeg. Simmer gently for 5 minutes, stirring occasionally. Stir in ¼ cup Sriracha. While whisking continuously, add 1½ cups grated Cheddar cheese, one handful at a time. Once the cheese has melted, add the cooked cauliflower and stir gently until evenly coated. Transfer to the prepared casserole dish. Top with ⅓ cup grated Parmigiano-Reggiano cheese and another ¼ cup grated Cheddar cheese. Spread the panko (cooked in butter rather than oil if you like) evenly over the top and bake as directed.

GF For the topping, substitute 2 cups of rice squares cereal (such as Rice Chex) for the panko. Put the cereal in a large ziplock bag and gently roll over it with a rolling pin until the cereal is coarsely crushed into bits, resembling panko in texture. For the cheeze sauce, simply substitute gluten-free flour for the all-purpose flour.

CURRIED KALE AND SQUASH RISOTTO

Risotto, the king of rice dishes so often feared by home cooks, is actually pretty darn easy to make if you bake it. Screw that "stir constantly" crap; I've got things to do! If you can muster up the wherewithal to stir this version once every fifteen minutes for forty-five minutes—yes, a whopping three times—congrats in advance on becoming the newest member of the risotto cognoscenti. **MAKES 4 TO 6 SERVINGS**

Rice

- 2 tablespoons extra-virgin olive oil
- 1/2 red onion, diced
- 3 cloves garlic, minced
- 1 cup Arborio rice
- 1/4 cup Sriracha
- 1/2 cup dry white wine or malty amber ale (see sidebar)
- 3 to 4 cups vegetable stock, kept hot

Kale-Squash Topping

- 1 small butternut squash, seeded and cubed
- 1 bunch kale, stemmed and coarsely chopped
- 1/2 medium red onion, halved lengthwise and sliced
- 1 clove garlic, minced
- 2 tablespoons extra-virgin olive oil
- 1 1/2 tablespoons curry powder
  Salt and freshly ground black pepper

- 1/2 cup nutritional yeast flakes
  Salt and freshly ground black pepper
  Toasted pine nuts (see sidebar, page 53), for garnish (optional)

Preheat the oven to 350°F.

To prepare the rice, heat the oil in an ovenproof pot or Dutch oven over medium heat. Add the onion and sauté until softened, 5 to 7 minutes. Add the garlic and sauté just until fragrant, about 30 seconds. Stir in the rice and continue stirring until every grain is coated with oil and the rice has a nutty aroma, about 5 minutes. Add the Sriracha and stir until the rice is evenly coated. Pour in the white wine to deglaze the pan, using a wooden spoon to scrape up all the stubborn, tasty brown bits. Cook until the wine has almost entirely evaporated, 2 to 3 minutes. Add 1 1/2 cups of the hot stock and bring to a boil. Cover and transfer to the oven and bake for 15 minutes.

To make the topping, combine the butternut squash, kale, onion, garlic, oil, and curry powder in a large bowl and toss until well combined. Season generously with salt and pepper. Spread the mixture in an even layer in a large roasting pan or on a rimmed baking sheet.

Carefully remove the risotto from the oven and give it a healthy stir, then stir in another $1/2$ cup hot stock. Cover and return to the oven. Put the squash mixture in the oven, too.

Bake for 15 minutes, then remove the risotto from the oven once again. (Leave the veggies in to continue roasting.) Give the risotto a healthy stir, then stir in another $1/2$ cup of hot stock. Cover and return to the oven.

Bake for 15 minutes. Remove both vessels from the oven. The veggies should be fork-tender, and the rice should be creamy, with no trace of chalkiness. If the rice is still too firm or dry in the center of each grain, add another $1/2$ cup of hot stock. Stir, cover, and return to the oven for 15 minutes. (Keep the squash covered so it stays hot.) Once the texture is right, stir in another $1/2$ cup of hot stock and the nutritional yeast. Season the risotto and the squash mixture with salt and pepper to taste.

Serve on individual plates, creating a small divot in each mound of risotto. Fill the divot with the squash mixture, garnish with pine nuts, and serve immediately.

Ⓥ Feel free to substitute 2 tablespoons melted butter and $1/4$ cup grated Parmigiano-Reggiano cheese for the nutritional yeast flakes.

> **YO! BEER ME!** My good comrade, Anya, requested a recipe such as this risotto for the book. And I wouldn't be doing it any justice if I didn't include an option to use beer, which adds an awesome layer of flavor, in place of the traditional white wine. Anya's husband, Mike (who's a pretty wicked cook!), loves to make his "beersotto" with Chimay Grande Réserve. While this Belgian Trappist ale is fairly readily available, feel free to substitute any amber to dark brown malt-forward ale or porter. Avoid hoppy beers and big, thick stouts. (If gluten is an issue, be sure to choose a gluten-free beer.)

SRIRACHA SWEET POTATO SHEPHERD'S PIE

I didn't really appreciate shepherd's pie before trying the tempeh shepherd's pie at Stone Brewing World Bistro & Gardens, which I ate a *lot* of during recipe testing for my second book. This rendition definitely draws some influence from Stone, but I've added Sriracha (duh) and used sweet potatoes for the topping, with some chipotles thrown in to provide a smoky heat that puts it all over the top. **MAKES 6 TO 8 SERVINGS**

Topping

- 2 pounds sweet potatoes, peeled and quartered
- 1 head roasted garlic (see sidebar)
- 1/2 cup vegetable stock
- 2 tablespoons extra-virgin olive oil or coconut oil
- 2 chipotle chiles in adobo sauce, minced
- Salt and freshly ground black pepper

Filling

- 1 (8-ounce) package tempeh, crumbled
- 1/4 cup Sriracha
- 3 tablespoons Bragg Liquid Aminos or low-sodium soy sauce
- 1 tablespoon garlic powder
- 2 teaspoons ground cumin
- 3 tablespoons extra-virgin olive oil
- 1 small red onion, diced
- 2 carrots, diced
- 2 stalks celery, diced
- 1 small zucchini, diced
- 1/2 cup frozen or fresh peas
- 3 cloves garlic, minced

- 3 tablespoons tomato paste
- 1/2 cup vegetable stock
- Salt and freshly ground black pepper

Chopped fresh flat-leaf parsley, for garnish

To make the topping, put the sweet potatoes in a saucepan, add water to cover, and season with a generous amount of salt. Bring to a boil over high heat, then immediately lower the heat, cover, and simmer until the potatoes are fork-tender, 15 to 20 minutes. Drain well. Add the garlic, stock, oil, and chipotles and use a potato masher to puree the mixture and combine well. Add more stock or oil for a thinner consistency if desired. Season with salt and pepper to taste.

Preheat the oven to 350°F.

To make the filling, mix the tempeh, Sriracha, liquid aminos, garlic powder, and cumin in a bowl. Heat 2 tablespoons of the oil in a large cast-iron or nonstick skillet over medium heat. Add the onion, carrots, and celery and sauté for 3 minutes. Add the zucchini and sauté until all the veggies are softened, 3 to 4 minutes. Add the peas and garlic and sauté just until the garlic is fragrant, about 30 seconds. Move the vegetables toward the outer edge of the pan, creating a well in the center. Pour the remaining tablespoon of oil into the well and let it heat slightly. Add the tempeh mixture to the well and stir to coat with the oil. Add tomato paste and mix everything together. Cook for 1 minute, stirring constantly. Pour in the stock to deglaze the pan, using a wooden spoon to scrape up all the stubborn, tasty brown bits. Cook, stirring occasionally, until most of the moisture has evaporated, about 3 minutes. Season with salt and pepper to taste.

To assemble the dish, transfer the filling to a 9 by 13-inch baking pan and spread it in an even layer. Top with sweet potato mixture, spreading it evenly as well. Cover with aluminum foil and bake for 20 minutes. Serve immediately, garnished with parsley.

Ⓥ Feel free to sub cream or milk for the veggie stock in the sweet potatoes.

MAKE-AHEAD TIP You can assemble the shepherd's pie up to 2 days before serving. Cover with aluminum foil and refrigerate. When you're ready to cook it, bake, covered, at 350°F until heated through, 35 to 40 minutes.

ROASTED GARLIC

To roast garlic, preheat the oven to 350°F. Cut the top 1/4 inch off of a head of garlic, leaving the head intact but exposing the individual cloves of garlic. Place the garlic cut side up on a large sheet of aluminum foil, drizzle 1 tablespoon olive oil over the top, and season with a sprinkling of salt and pepper. Gather the foil up around the garlic, folding or twisting the top to seal. Bake for 1 hour, then let cool to room temperature. Squeeze the flesh out from the bottom up by hand, or use a fork to pull it out.

MAPLE-SRIRACHA ROASTED BRUSSELS SPROUTS WITH CRANBERRY WILD RICE

While I wish I could take all the credit for the unique blend of flavors here, the inspiration for the brussels sprouts came from a restaurant in NYC called the Vanderbilt. I was going to rework their recipe as a side dish, but after taking my first bite of this new version, I realized that serving the brussels sprouts atop my favorite wild rice dish would create a stunning entrée. **MAKES 4 TO 6 SERVINGS**

Cranberry Wild Rice

2 tablespoons extra-virgin olive oil

1 small red onion, diced

3 cloves garlic, minced

2 bay leaves

1 1/2 cups wild rice

3 1/2 cups vegetable stock

1/2 cup unsweetened dried cranberries

1/4 cup chopped raw walnuts or pecans

2 tablespoons minced fresh rosemary

Salt and freshly ground black pepper

Brussels Sprouts

1/2 cup Grade B maple syrup or raw agave nectar

3 tablespoons extra-virgin olive oil

3 tablespoons Sriracha

1 1/2 tablespoons Bragg Liquid Aminos or low-sodium soy sauce

Juice of 1 lime

1 pound brussels sprouts, trimmed and halved lengthwise

Chopped fresh flat-leaf parsley, for garnish (optional)

To make the rice, heat the oil in a large Dutch oven or pot over medium-high heat. Add the onion and sauté until softened, 5 to 7 minutes. Add the garlic and bay leaves and sauté just until the garlic is fragrant, about 30 seconds. Add the rice and stir until evenly coated. Continue to cook, stirring occasionally, until the rice is slightly toasted and has a nutty aroma, about 3 minutes. Pour in 1 cup of the stock to deglaze the pan, using a wooden spoon to scrape up all the stubborn, tasty brown bits. Add the remaining 2 1/2 cups of stock and the cranberries. Bring to a boil, then immediately lower the heat, cover, and simmer until the rice is tender and some of the grains have popped, 50 to 60 minutes. Uncover and fluff with a fork. Simmer for 5 minutes, stirring occasionally. Remove from the heat and drain off any excess liquid.

CONTINUED

While the rice is cooking, prepare the brussels sprouts. Preheat the oven to 375°F. In a large bowl, combine the maple syrup, oil, Sriracha, liquid aminos, and lime juice and whisk until well blended. Add the brussels sprouts and toss until evenly coated. Using a slotted spoon, transfer the brussels sprouts to a nonstick or parchment-lined rimmed baking sheet or a large cast-iron skillet and spread them in a single layer. Reserve any liquid left in the bowl. Bake the brussels sprouts for about 25 minutes, until tender and browned.

To finish the rice and serve, add the walnuts to the rice without stirring. Cover and let stand for 5 minutes. Add the rosemary and fluff with a fork to combine. Season with salt and pepper to taste. Serve the brussels sprouts over the rice, garnished with a healthy drizzle of the reserved maple-Sriracha dressing and a sprinkling of parsley.

V You can use honey in place of the maple syrup if you wish. Raw orange blossom honey would be especially nice.

BRAISED EGGPLANT TAGINE WITH SRIRACHA HARISSA AND MINT-COCONUT CREMA

A tagine is a traditional Northern African stew, typically cooked in an earthenware vessel called, well, a tagine. These vessels have a flat, round base and a cone- or dome-shaped lid, which promotes condensation of steam, helping retain moisture in the finished dish. If you've got a tagine, great! If not, a Dutch oven or casserole will work just fine. Make sure to use harissa paste, not powder, or make your own harissa (see sidebar, page 90). **MAKES 4 TO 6 SERVINGS**

Mint-Coconut Crema

- 1 (14-ounce) can coconut milk (*not* the low-fat or light variety)
  Juice of 1 to 2 limes
- 2 tablespoons chopped fresh mint
- 1 tablespoon white or yellow miso (optional)
- 1/2 teaspoon kosher salt

Sriracha Harissa Sauce

- 1/4 cup Sriracha
- 1/4 cup harissa paste (see sidebar, page 90)

Tagine

- 2 tablespoons extra-virgin olive oil
- 1 large red onion, halved lengthwise and sliced
- 1 green bell pepper, diced
- 1 large eggplant, diced large
- 3 cloves garlic, minced
- 3 tablespoons *ras el hanout* (see sidebar, page 91)

- 2 1/2 cups vegetable stock
- 1/4 cup raisins
- 1 cup brown lentils, soaked in water for 2 hours
- 1 lemon
  Salt and freshly ground black pepper
  Chopped fresh flat-leaf parsley, for garnish

To make the crema, refrigerate the can of coconut milk for at least 4 hours. Open the can and scoop out all the creamy goodness that's solidified in there into a bowl, leaving any liquid behind in the can. Add the juice of 1 lime, mint, miso, and salt. Mix until smooth, with the consistency of sour cream. Taste and season with more salt or lime juice, if desired. Transfer to an airtight container and refrigerate until serving time.

CONTINUED

To make the harissa sauce, mix the Sriracha and harissa paste in a small bowl. Cover and set aside.

To make the tagine, heat the oil in a large tagine or Dutch oven over medium heat. Add the onion, bell pepper, and eggplant and sauté until the onions are softened, about 7 minutes. Add the garlic and *ras el hanout* and sauté until the seasoning is slightly toasted, about 1 minute. Pour in

HARISSA

Harissa is an amazeballs chile paste that hails from Morocco. It shouldn't be too difficult to find, but if you can't locate it or simply dig the idea of making your own, here's my favorite way to do it! For the chiles, I like a mixture of ancho, guajillo, chipotle, and/or pasilla. **MAKES ABOUT 1½ CUPS**

6 large dried chiles
2 roasted red bell peppers
Juice of 1 lemon
2 cloves of garlic
2 teaspoons cumin
½ teaspoon ground cayenne pepper
½ teaspoon coriander
¼ cup extra-virgin olive oil
Salt and freshly ground black pepper

Soak the chiles in ½ cup boiling water until they are fully reconstituted, about 15 minutes. Carefully remove them from the soaking liquid. Trim the top from the chiles and discard along with the seeds.

Place the chiles into the bowl of a food processor or high-powered blender, along with the bell peppers, lemon juice, garlic, cumin, cayenne, and coriander. Blend until a coarse paste forms. With the processor running, slowly drizzle in the olive oil through the feed tube. Season with salt and pepper, to taste. Store refrigerated in an airtight container, and use within 1 month for best flavor.

1 cup of the stock to deglaze the pan, using a wooden spoon to scrape up all the stubborn, tasty brown bits. Stir in the remaining 1¹/₂ cups of stock and the raisins. Drain the lentils and stir them in. Bring to a boil, then immediately lower the heat, cover, and simmer until lentils and eggplant are tender, 25 to 30 minutes. Mince the zest of half a lemon, then juice the entire lemon. Stir the zest and lemon juice into the tagine. Season with salt and pepper to taste. Garnish with parsley and serve family-style, with the crema and harissa sauce in bowls alongside.

Ⓥ For the crema, feel free to substitute ³/₄ cup plain whole-milk yogurt (not low-fat or nonfat) for the coconut, cashews, lime juice, miso, and salt. Simply stir the chopped mint into the yogurt.

GF In addition to making sure the miso and vegetable stock are gluten-free, as usual, check the harissa label. Some brands include ingredients that contain gluten. If you can't find a gluten-free variety, make your own using the recipe on the opposite page.

RAS EL HANOUT *Ras el hanout* is a traditional Moroccan spice blend. Its name loosely translates to "head (or top) of the shop," indicating that its ingredients include some of the finest spices a given vendor offers. It adds an interesting touch when substituted for cumin in recipes, such as Sriracha-Cucumber Hummus (page 22) and Five-Alarm Black Bean Soup with Cilantro-Coconut Crema (page 34). Look for it at Middle Eastern markets or online, or make your own blend. Here are some guidelines, but please feel free to improvise, as the mixture is different in every household according to taste and can contain anywhere from a handful of different ingredients to upward of fifty. For a basic *ras el hanout*, combine 2 teaspoons each of: ground cinnamon, coriander, ginger, black pepper, and turmeric, plus 1 teaspoon each of: ground nutmeg, allspice, and cayenne pepper.

SPICY CALIFORNIA ROLLS

Since the basis of a California roll is already mock crab (usually made from a much cheaper fish called pollock), I have no misgivings about making mock mock crab using garbanzo beans. Mixing in nori brings a briny flavor from the sea, while Old Bay Seasoning adds depth and character that will make you oh-so-happy. Y'know . . . as opposed to crabby. **MAKES 4 TO 6 SERVINGS**

Sushi Rice

- 2 cups sushi rice or short-grain white rice
- 2 cups water
- 2 tablespoons rice vinegar (not the seasoned variety)
- 2 tablespoons sugar
- 2 teaspoons fine sea salt

Mock Crab

- 1 sheet nori
- 1³/₄ cup cooked garbanzo beans, or 1 (15-ounce) can, drained
- ¹/₄ cup Sriracha
- 3 tablespoons vegan mayonnaise or Flax Mayonnaise (page 17)
- 1 carrot, grated and then minced
- 1 clove garlic, minced
- ¹/₂ teaspoon Old Bay Seasoning or seasoned salt
  Salt and freshly ground black pepper

- 2 large, ripe Hass avocados
  Juice of ¹/₂ lemon
- 8 sheets nori
- ¹/₄ to ¹/₂ cup toasted black sesame seeds (see sidebar, page 53)

- 1 large English cucumber, peeled and julienned
- 1 large carrot, julienned
  Pickled ginger, for serving
  Wasabi, for serving
  Soy sauce, for serving

To prepare the rice, put the rice in a large bowl and cover with cool water. Swirl around, drain, and repeat until the water runs clear. Combine the rice and water in a small saucepan set over medium-high heat. Bring to a boil, then immediately lower the heat as low as possible. Cover and simmer for 15 minutes. Remove from the heat and let stand, covered, for 10 minutes. (For best results, use a rice cooker to cook the rice).

In a small bowl, combine the vinegar, sugar, and salt and stir until the salt and sugar have dissolved. Transfer the rice to a nonmetallic bowl (wooden if available). Drizzle in the vinegar mixture while stirring with a wooden spoon until the rice is evenly coated. Let cool to room temperature—don't refrigerate.

To make the mock crab, break up the nori. Process it in a spice grinder or mortar and pestle to create a fine powder. (Alternatively, mince it as finely as possible with a knife.) Transfer to a small bowl.

In the bowl of a food processor, combine the garbanzo beans, Sriracha, vegan mayonnaise, carrot, garlic, and Old Bay Seasoning and pulse until the mixture comes together and has a coarse texture, with plenty of medium-size chunky pieces. Transfer to a bowl and stir in $1/2$ teaspoon of the powdered nori. Season with salt, pepper, and more powdered nori to taste. Cover and let sit at room temperature while the rest of the assembly ingredients come together. (This can be made up to 2 days in advance and kept in the refrigerator. Remove from the fridge 30 minutes before use.)

To assemble the nori rolls, peel, pit, and slice the avocados. Sprinkle the lemon juice over the avocado slices to help prevent browning. Cover a bamboo sushi mat with plastic wrap. Place one sheet of nori on a work surface with the shiny side facing down. Lightly dampen your fingers and use them to spread about $1/2$ cup of the rice in a thin, even layer over the entire surface of the nori. Sprinkle $1/2$ to 1 tablespoon of the black sesame seeds over the rice. Place the plastic-wrapped rolling mat on top of the rice, then carefully flip the assembly so that the mat is on the bottom and the nori is on top. On the end closest to you, spread about one-eighth of the mock crab in a thin line across the nori. Place about one-eighth of the avocado, cucumber, and carrot in thin lines alongside the mock crab.

Use the sushi mat to roll the rice-covered nori around the fillings, beginning at the end closest to you, keeping the filling in place with your fingers. With each turn, use the mat to shape and tighten the roll. Set the finished roll aside and cover with a small piece of plastic wrap, which will keep it moist and aid in slicing the roll later. Repeat to make 7 more rolls. Dip a sharp chef's knife in water, then cut each roll in half. Make two more cuts out on each side to yield a total of 6 pieces per roll. Discard the plastic wrap. Serve immediately, with the pickled ginger, wasabi, and soy sauce alongside.

CAJUN QUINOA CAKES WITH LEMON-DILL-SRIRACHA RÉMOULADE

I want to believe that I'm quinoa's biggest cheerleader, but it seems every time I talk to someone about it—which is more often than I care to admit—the response is almost always "*OMG!* I friggin' *love* quinoa!" After you taste these quinoa cakes, I'm willing to venture that you'll soon be on the hunt for other awesome quinoa recipes. That is, if you aren't already . . . **MAKES 4 TO 6 SERVINGS**

1 cup quinoa
2 cups vegetable stock or water

Lemon-Dill-Sriracha Rémoulade
1 lemon
$^1/_2$ cup vegan mayonnaise or Flax Mayonnaise (page 17)
$^1/_4$ cup Sriracha
3 tablespoons chopped fresh dill
1 large clove garlic, minced
Salt and freshly ground black pepper

1 tablespoon ground flaxseeds
3 tablespoons water
$^1/_4$ cup whole wheat or all-purpose flour
$^1/_2$ red onion, diced
2 stalks celery, diced
$^1/_2$ green bell pepper, diced
3 cloves garlic, minced
Salt and freshly ground black pepper
2 tablespoons extra-virgin olive oil
Chopped fresh dill, for garnish

In a small saucepan, combine the quinoa and stock. Bring to a boil over medium heat, then immediately lower the heat, cover, and simmer until the liquid is absorbed, about 15 minutes. Transfer to a bowl, fluff with a fork, and let cool to room temperature.

Meanwhile, prepare the rémoulade. Mince the zest of half the lemon, then juice the lemon. In a small bowl, mix the vegan mayonnaise, Sriracha, dill, garlic, and lemon juice and zest. Season with salt and pepper to taste. Cover and set aside. (This can be made up to 2 days in advance and kept in the refrigerator.)

In a small bowl, mix the flaxseeds and water and let sit for several minutes, until a gel forms. Add to the quinoa, along with the flour, onion, celery, bell pepper, and garlic. Season generously with salt and pepper and mix well. The mixture should be moist enough to stick together and slightly tacky. Adjust with water or flour to achieve the proper consistency. Form into 8 to 12 patties about $1/2$ inch thick. (The patties can be made 1 day in advance and kept in the refrigerator.)

Preheat the oven to 200°F. Put a wire rack atop a baking sheet or line a baking sheet with foil. Put the baking sheet in the oven.

Heat the oil in a large cast-iron or nonstick skillet over medium heat. Add the patties and cook until browned on the bottom, about 4 minutes. Gently flip and cook until the other side is browned, 4 to 5 minutes. Transfer to the wire rack in the oven to keep warm. Once all of the quinoa cakes are cooked, serve immediately, garnishing each with a generous dollop of rémoulade and a sprinkling of dill.

(V) For the quinoa cakes, feel free to substitute 1 large beaten egg for the flax and water mixture.

GETTING BAKED If you want to make a larger batch of these, or if you're just trying to cut down on frying, you can also bake these bad boys! Simply arrange them in a single layer on a lightly greased baking sheet and bake at 400°F until golden brown and heated through, about 25 minutes total, gently flipping once about halfway through.

ULTIMATE SRIRACHA VEGGIE BURGER

Remove any preconceived notions you may have about veggie burgers. This is not some frostbitten hockey puck of a patty that's been sitting in your grocer's freezer section for an eternity. Nay! This is a delicious handmade treasure, bursting with moisture and flavor thanks to the mixture of black beans and fresh mushrooms. Topped with arugula, roasted red bell pepper, avocado, and aioli seasoned with cumin and Sriracha, all I can say is . . . you're welcome in advance! **MAKES 4 SERVINGS**

Sriracha-Cumin Aioli

- $1/4$ cup vegan mayonnaise or Flax Mayonnaise (page 17)
- 2 tablespoons Sriracha
- 2 teaspoons ground cumin
- 1 clove garlic, minced

Patties

- $1^3/4$ cups cooked black beans, or 1 (15-ounce) can, rinsed and drained
- 1 tablespoon ground flaxseeds
- 3 tablespoons water
- 3 tablespoons extra-virgin olive oil
- 1 cup diced red onion
- 8 ounces cremini or button mushrooms, thinly sliced
- 2 tablespoons minced fresh cilantro
- 2 cloves garlic, peeled
- $1/4$ cup Sriracha
- 1 tablespoon Bragg Liquid Aminos or low-sodium soy sauce
- 2 teaspoons freshly ground black pepper
- 1 to $1^1/2$ cups fresh bread crumbs

- 4 sesame seed buns or ciabatta rolls
  Arugula leaves, for serving
- 1 roasted red bell pepper, cut into long strips
- 1 ripe Hass avocado, pitted and sliced just before serving

To make the aioli, combine the vegan mayonnaise, Sriracha, cumin, and garlic in a small bowl and stir until well combined. Cover and refrigerate until ready to use.

To make the patties, spread the rinsed and drained beans in a single layer on a clean kitchen towel or paper towels. Cover with an additional towel or more paper towels and pat dry.

In a small bowl, mix the flaxseeds and water and let sit for several minutes, until a gel forms.

Heat the oil in a large cast-iron or non-stick skillet over medium-high heat. Add the

CONTINUED

Main Dishes   97

onion and sauté until softened, 5 to 7 minutes. Add the mushrooms and sauté until they have given off their moisture and begin to brown, 5 to 7 minutes. Remove from the heat and let cool slightly.

Transfer to a food processor and add the beans, flaxseed gel, cilantro, garlic, Sriracha, liquid aminos, pepper, and 1 cup of bread crumbs. Pulse just until combined, with some chunky bean bits still intact. Form the mixture into 4 patties and let sit while you preheat the grill. If the patties aren't firm enough to hold their shape, incorporate additional bread crumbs by hand, then form into patties again.

Lightly oil a grill or grill pan and preheat to medium-high heat. Using a metal spatula, gently transfer the patties onto the grill. Cook until well browned on both sides, about 10 minutes total, gently flipping once about halfway through. Lightly toast buns in the last minute or two of cooking if desired.

To assemble the burger, spread the aioli on the top and bottom of each bun. Load each up with a patty, a small handful of arugula, and one-fourth of the red bell pepper and avocado. Serve immediately.

GF Substitute almond flour for bread crumbs. Use gluten-free hamburger buns, or wrap your topped burgers in large leaves of iceberg, Boston, or Bibb lettuce.

JACKFRUIT "PULLED PORK" SAMMICHES WITH PICKLED RED ONION

I first enjoyed fresh jackfruit (which is one helluva treat) at my friend Phi's house. Sadly, canned jackfruit packed in syrup pales in comparison. And then there's canned young jackfruit packed in brine, a product that doesn't sound anywhere near as tasty. When shredded, however, it makes an excellent stand-in for pulled pork, right down to the texture. I discovered this novel substitution at the delightful vegan SoCal food truck Seabirds, and I've been hooked ever since. It might take a little searching, but you should be able to find canned young jackfruit in brine at Asian markets or online. **MAKES 4 TO 6 SERVINGS**

Pickled Red Onion

- 1 large red onion, halved lengthwise and thinly sliced
- 1 cup apple cider vinegar
- 3 tablespoons sugar
- 2 teaspoons fine sea salt
- 6 whole black peppercorns (optional)

Jackfruit "Pulled Pork"

- 3 tablespoons extra-virgin olive oil
- 1 small red onion, diced
- 4 cloves garlic, minced
- 1 tablespoon smoked paprika
- 1 tablespoon ground cumin
- 1 teaspoon dry mustard
- 3 tablespoons tomato paste
- $^1/_4$ to $^1/_2$ cup Sriracha
- $^1/_4$ cup water
- 3 tablespoons light brown sugar

- 2 (20-ounce) cans jackfruit packed in brine
  Salt and freshly ground black pepper

  Hamburger buns or rolls, for serving
  Sliced ripe Hass avocado, for serving

To make the pickled onion, put the onion in a large saucepan and add water to cover. Bring to a boil over high heat. Boil for 1 minute, then drain well. Transfer to a small bowl or a glass jar. In the same saucepan, combine the vinegar, sugar, salt, and peppercorns. Bring to a boil over high heat, then immediately remove from the heat. Pour over the onion. Let cool to room temperature, then cover and refrigerate for at least 1 hour before serving. Stored in the refrigerator, it will keep for 1 month.

CONTINUED

To make the "pulled pork," preheat the oven to 350°F.

Heat the oil in a large cast-iron or non-stick skillet over medium heat. Add the onion and sauté until softened, 5 to 7 minutes. Add the garlic and sauté just until fragrant, about 30 seconds. Add paprika, cumin, and mustard and sauté until the spices are toasted, about 3 minutes. Add the tomato paste and cook, stirring constantly, for 1 minute. Stir in $1/4$ cup Sriracha, the water, and the brown sugar. Bring to a simmer, then lower the heat, cover, and simmer for 5 minutes. Uncover and cook, stirring occasionally, until the mixture has the consistency of barbecue sauce, about 4 minutes. Remove from the heat. Taste and add more Sriracha if desired.

Drain the jackfruit and rinse under cool running water to reduce the saltiness. Transfer to a large bowl and use two forks to pull the jackfruit into shreds. Add the Sriracha mixture and toss until the jackfruit is evenly coated. Transfer to a nonstick or parchment-lined rimmed baking sheet. Bake for about 20 minutes, until the jackfruit firms up and the sauce dries slightly, adhering to the jackfruit. Season with salt and pepper to taste.

To assemble the sandwiches, divide the "pulled pork" among the buns. Top with avocado slices and pickled onion. Serve immediately.

GF Substitute gluten-free hamburger buns, or wrap the "pulled pork" in gluten-free tortillas or large leaves of iceberg, Boston, or Bibb lettuce.

> **OVER THE TOP TIP** If you're crazy and want yet another spicy topping, slap some Sriracha Broccoli Slaw (page 47) on top of this beast for a truly invigorating (and extra-delicious) experience.

SAM'S JAMAICAN JERK GARBANZO SLIDERS WITH MANGO-CUCUMBER RELISH

My good friend Samantha Loveira is no stranger to making delicious plant-based food, something I learned shortly after starting to work with her at Stone Brewing Co. When I dropped a clue that I was working on a follow-up Sriracha cookbook for veggie lovers, she was quick to offer help with recipe testing. I asked if she'd be interested in developing a recipe of her own to contribute; she jumped at the chance, and this is the delightful result. **MAKES 4 TO 6 SERVINGS**

Relish

- 1 large mango, julienned
- $1/2$ Persian cucumber, or $1/4$ English cucumber, julienned
- $1/4$ small red onion, thinly sliced
- 1 tablespoon minced fresh mint
- Juice of 1 lime
- 1 tablespoon extra-virgin olive oil
- Salt and freshly ground black pepper

Jerk Sauce

- $1/4$ cup Sriracha
- 2 tablespoons Bragg Liquid Aminos or low-sodium soy sauce
- Juice of 1 lime
- 4 green onions, white and green parts, coarsely chopped
- 2 cloves garlic, peeled
- 1 tablespoon light brown sugar
- 1 tablespoon minced fresh thyme, or $1^{1}/2$ teaspoons dried
- 2 teaspoons ground allspice
- 1 teaspoon grated fresh ginger or ground ginger

- $1/2$ teaspoon ground nutmeg
- $1/4$ teaspoon ground cinnamon
- $1/2$ cup vegan mayonnaise or Flax Mayonnaise (page 17)
- Salt and freshly ground black pepper

Patties

- 1 tablespoon ground flaxseeds
- 3 tablespoons water
- $1^{3}/4$ cups cooked garbanzo beans, or 1 (15-ounce) can, drained
- $1/2$ cup panko bread crumbs
- $1/2$ red onion, minced
- $1/2$ red bell pepper, minced
- 1 small carrot, grated
- 1 clove garlic, minced
- Salt and freshly ground black pepper

- 2 tablespoons extra-virgin olive oil

- 12 slider buns, or 4 hamburger buns
- Fresh cilantro leaves, for serving

To make the relish, put the mango, cucumber, onion, mint, lime juice, and oil in a bowl and toss until well combined. Season with salt and pepper to taste. Cover and refrigerate for at least 30 minutes. (This can be made up to 3 days in advance.)

To make the sauce, combine the Sriracha, liquid aminos, lime juice, green onions, garlic, brown sugar, thyme, allspice, ginger, nutmeg, and cinnamon in a food processor. Process until a smooth, thick sauce forms. If it's too thick, add a bit of water. Set aside half of the sauce to include in the patties. Mix the other half with vegan mayonnaise and season with salt and pepper to taste. Cover and refrigerate until needed. (This can be made up to 3 days in advance.)

To make the patties, mix the flaxseeds and water in a small bowl and let sit for several minutes, until a gel forms.

In a medium bowl, crush the garbanzo beans with a potato masher or fork until they have a coarse texture, with plenty of medium-size chunky pieces. Add the flaxseed gel, panko, onion, bell pepper, carrot, garlic, and the reserved jerk sauce (the half without mayo). Mix well, then season with salt and pepper to taste. Divide the mixture into 12 equal portions, roll them into balls, and then flatten slightly into disks about 1 inch thick. (If you prefer full-size patties or can't find slider buns, make 4 regular-size patties.)

Remove the relish from the fridge to take some of the chill off. Heat the oil in a large cast-iron or nonstick skillet over medium heat. Add the patties and cook until nicely browned on both sides, 8 to 10 minutes total, gently flipping once about halfway through.

To assemble the sliders, spread the jerk sauce (the half with mayo) on the top and bottom of each bun. Load each bun with a patty, some of the relish, and a few cilantro leaves. Serve immediately, with any leftover relish offered on the side.

GF Substitute almond flour for the bread crumbs. Gluten-free slider buns may be a little difficult to come by. Feel free to make your own, or just make 4 regular-size patties and use gluten-free hamburger buns. Another alternative is to wrap the patties and condiments in large leaves of iceberg, Boston, or Bibb lettuce.

DIOS MIO TAMALES

When I made the switch to a plant-based diet, I thought tamales were out of my life forever, since they're traditionally made with lard. But I had a vegan tamale at Tamara's Tamales on the Westside of Los Angeles that rocked my world and sent me to my kitchen to create my own version. *Dios mio* means "my god" *en español*, as in "oh my god," which you'll undoubtedly be exclaiming when you taste these, partially because of the awesome flavor combo, and partially because of the heat that sneaks up after a few bites. For a fantastic meal, serve the tamales with Spanish rice, black beans, guacamole, and salsa—preferably pico de gallo or salsa verde. For extra zing, serve them with Sriracha-Mango Guacamole (page 23). **MAKES 6 TO 8 SERVINGS**

Masa Dough

- 4 cups masa harina
- 2 teaspoons baking powder
- 1 teaspoon fine sea salt
- 1 head roasted garlic (see sidebar, page 85)
- 1/4 cup minced fresh cilantro
- 4 cups vegetable stock
- 1/2 cup Sriracha
- 1/4 cup extra-virgin olive oil

Filling

- 2 tablespoons extra-virgin olive oil
- 1 red onion, diced
- 8 ounces cremini or button mushrooms, thinly sliced
- 1 green bell pepper, diced
- 1 small zucchini, diced
- 3 cloves garlic, minced
- 2 tablespoons ground cumin

Kernels from 2 ears fresh sweet corn, roasted (see page 106)

- 1 bunch spinach, stemmed, or 1 (10-ounce) package frozen spinach, thawed and drained
  Salt and freshly ground black pepper

- 2 (6-ounce) packages corn husks, soaked in warm water for at least 1 hour

To make the dough, combine the masa harina, baking powder, and salt in a large bowl (or the bowl of a stand mixer fitted with the paddle attachment) and mix well. Add the roasted garlic, cilantro, stock, Sriracha, and oil and whip with a handheld electric mixer or stand mixer until soft and fluffy, 3 to 5 minutes. Cover and set aside.

CONTINUED

To make the filling, heat the oil in a large Dutch oven or pot over medium-high heat. Add the onion, mushrooms, bell pepper, and zucchini and sauté until softened, 5 to 7 minutes. Add the garlic, cumin, and corn and sauté just until the garlic is fragrant, about 30 seconds. Add the spinach and sauté until completely wilted and its moisture has evaporated, about 5 minutes. Season with salt and pepper to taste. Let cool to room temperature.

To assemble and steam the tamales, remove the corn husks from their soaking water. Lay a large corn husk or two overlapping small husks on a work surface. Spread 2 tablespoons of dough down the center, leaving a $1/2$-inch border on each side and a 3-inch border on the top and bottom. Top with a generous tablespoonful of the filling, followed by another tablespoon of the masa. Fold up the sides of the husk and pull the top and bottom in to fully encase the filling.

Seal the tamale using by tying either kitchen twine or strips of corn husk around it. This needn't be excessively tight, as the tamales will expand during cooking.

Loosely pack the tamales in a large steamer basket and steam them until they expand and feel firm to the touch, about 1 hour, checking the water level periodically and adding more if needed. Serve immediately.

> **ROASTED CORN 101** To roast corn on the cob, remove the husks and set the corn over a direct flame (on a preheated grill or over a gas burner). Cook until the kernels begin to blacken, turning every few minutes until evenly roasted. Enjoy smeared with a little Sriracha Aioli (page 17) and sprinkled with a pinch of nutritional yeast flakes, or cut the kernels from the cob to use in recipes.

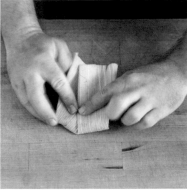

BEER-BATTERED FRIED AVOCADO TACOS WITH SRIRACHA CURTIDO

This recipe melds together a few of my favorite things: beer, avocado, Sriracha, and curtido, an incredibly tangy slaw hailing from El Salvador—spiked with Sriracha in this version. Many thanks to my friend chef Alex Carballo at Stone Brewing World Bistro & Gardens in San Diego for introducing me to beer-battered fried avocado tacos, a fantastic culinary treat. To round out the meal, serve with Spanish-style rice and black beans. **MAKES 4 SERVINGS**

Curtido

- 1/2 head green cabbage, shredded (about 4 cups)
- 1 small red onion, halved lengthwise and thinly sliced
- 1 large carrot, grated
- 1/2 cup water
- 1/2 cup apple cider vinegar
- 1/4 cup Sriracha
- 2 teaspoons dried Mexican oregano
- 2 teaspoons sugar
- 2 teaspoons fine sea salt

Beer-Battered Fried Avocados

- 2 cups strong amber ale (such as Arrogant Bastard Ale or Lagunitas Brown Shugga')
- 2 cups all-purpose flour
- 2 tablespoons garlic powder
- 2 teaspoons baking powder
- 2 teaspoons fine sea salt
- 1 teaspoon freshly ground black pepper

- 2 cups panko bread crumbs
- 2 large, ripe Hass avocados
  Extra-virgin olive oil or vegetable oil, for frying

- 8 or 16 small corn tortillas, warmed
  Fresh cilantro leaves, for garnish

To make the curtido, boil about 4 cups of water. Put the cabbage, onion, and carrot in a large mixing bowl and toss to combine. Pour in the boiling water and let stand for 5 minutes. Drain well. In a small saucepan, combine the 1/2 cup water, vinegar, Sriracha, oregano, sugar, and salt. Bring to a boil over high heat. Remove from the heat and stir to ensure that the sugar and salt have dissolved. Pour over the drained cabbage

CONTINUED

mixture and toss to combine. Let cool to room temperature, then cover and refrigerate until ready to use. (This can be made up to 1 week in advance and gets better after it's been sitting for a day or two.)

To make the fried avocados, put the ale, flour, garlic powder, baking powder, salt, and pepper in a bowl and whisk to combine. Prepare a deep fryer by filling it with oil to the manufacturer's suggested fill level. (Alternatively, use a wide, deep cast-iron or other heavy pan with oil to a depth of 2 to 3 inches, but no more than halfway up the side of the pan.) Heat the oil to 375°F. Spread the panko in a shallow baking dish. Cut the avocados in half, remove the pit, and scoop out the flesh, keeping it intact. Slice each half into four pieces. Dunk the slices into the ale mixture, shake off any excess, and then roll each piece in the panko. Carefully lower into the oil and fry until deep golden brown and crispy, 3 to 5 minutes. Remove with a slotted spoon and immediately season lightly with salt and pepper.

Now assemble the tacos. I like to stack 2 tortillas per taco, but you're welcome to use only 1 if that's your preference. Either way, top with 2 hot avocado slices. Using tongs, lift a big mound of the curtido from its pickling bath, give it a quick shake to ditch some of the liquid, and pile it atop the avocado. Garnish with cilantro and serve immediately.

(V) A little Cotija cheese crumbled on top would be delicious.

GF If you're able to source a gluten-free amber or golden beer that you enjoy, by all means, use it! Alternatively, you can use gluten-free vegetable stock. For the panko, substitute 2 cups of rice squares cereal (such as Rice Chex). Put the cereal in a large ziplock bag and gently roll over it with a rolling pin until the cereal is coarsely crushed, with pieces resembling panko in texture.

PENNE PUTTANESCA WITH CHARRED BROCCOLINI

Charred broccolini is one of the greatest things on earth. There's a spot in San Diego called Tiger!Tiger! Tavern that makes it in a wood-fired oven, and I could probably eat about ten pounds of it in a sitting if I put my mind to it. Behold my attempt to recreate that same glory using a broiler. I decided to combine it with one of my favorite pasta preparations, and the pairing is awesome! **MAKES 4 TO 6 SERVINGS**

4 tablespoons extra-virgin olive oil

1 small red onion, halved lengthwise and sliced

1 carrot, grated

4 cloves garlic, minced

2 bay leaves

2 tablespoons tomato paste

2 (28-ounce) cans whole tomatoes, undrained

¼ cup Sriracha

1 cup pitted kalamata olives

1 tablespoon nonpareil capers (optional)

Salt and freshly ground black pepper

1 pound penne pasta

1 pound broccolini

Juice of ½ lemon

Chopped fresh flat-leaf parsley, for garnish

Heat 2 tablespoons of the oil in a large cast-iron skillet or Dutch oven over medium heat. Add the onion and sauté until softened, 5 to 7 minutes. Stir in the carrot, three-quarters of the garlic, and bay leaves and sauté just until the garlic is fragrant, about 30 seconds. Add the tomato paste and cook, stirring constantly, for 1 minute. Crush the tomatoes with your hands and add them (with their liquid) to the skillet. Stir in the Sriracha, olives, and capers. Bring to a boil, then immediately lower the heat and simmer, stirring occasionally, for 45 minutes. Discard the bay leaves. Season with salt and pepper to taste.

About 20 minutes before the sauce is ready, bring a large pot of salted water to a

CONTINUED

boil over high heat. Preheat a grill, grill pan, or broiler to high heat. Put the broccolini in a bowl, drizzle with remaining 2 tablespoons of oil, add the remaining garlic, and toss until evenly coated. Season with salt and pepper.

Stir the penne into the boiling water, lower the heat to medium, and cook until just tender. Meanwhile, spread the broccolini in a single layer on the grill or a broiler pan. Cook until tender and lightly charred, about 7 minutes total, gently flipping once about halfway through. Remove from the heat and sprinkle with the lemon juice.

Drain the pasta well. Return it to the pot, add the sauce, and toss gently until well mixed. Serve immediately, garnished with parsley and topped with the broccolini.

GF Use gluten-free pasta in place of traditional pasta, or substitute steamed or roasted cauliflower florets for the pasta.

DESSERTS
AND
DRINKS

WATERMELON-SRIRACHA SANGRIA

So, a funny thing happened to me on the way to this recipe. You see, when *The Sriracha Cookbook* first came out, a mention of Sriracha Sangria somehow got on the press release, though I swear I'd never brought up such a concoction. Ever. But lo and behold, it seemed as though everyone was mentioning it: "Ooh! I can't wait to try it!" and the like. The only problem was that it didn't exist. But now, in a delectable display of supply and demand, I made a rockin' recipe for Sriracha Sangria, with the wonderful addition of everyone's favorite summertime treat: watermelon. It's procrastination in a glass.

MAKES 6 TO 8 SERVINGS

8 cups cubed seedless watermelon

1 (750 ml) bottle dry unoaked white wine (such as Sauvignon Blanc or Pinot Grigio)

$1/4$ cup Calvados, light rum, or brandy

$1/4$ cup sugar

3 tablespoons Sriracha

2 limes, thinly sliced

12 fluid ounces natural ginger ale (such as Reed's Original Ginger Brew)

Ice cubes, for serving

Fresh mint sprigs, for garnish

In a blender, puree 6 cups of the watermelon. Strain into a large pitcher. Add the wine, Calvados, sugar, Sriracha, lime slices, and remaining 2 cups of watermelon. Cover and refrigerate for at least 2 hours. (This can be made up to 2 days in advance.)

When ready to serve, give the mixture a healthy stir, then pour in the ginger ale. Put a few ice cubes in each glass, then fill with the sangria, making sure to get some lime and watermelon goodies in everyone's cup. Garnish with a sprig of mint and serve immediately.

MANGO-SRIRACHA MARGARITA

This may be the literal translation of sugar, spice, and everything nice. Sure, we can disagree on how nice you think tequila is the morning after, but in the moment, you know there's nothing quite like a nice, slushy margarita. It's best to find an unaged blanco or silver tequila for this recipe, though a young reposado would also work fine. If you *really* don't care for tequila, simply substitute rum and enjoy a fancy little daiquiri instead. Either way, your summer drinks will never be the same. **MAKES 4 SERVINGS**

1 (10-ounce) package frozen mango chunks

³/₄ cup freshly squeezed orange juice

¹/₂ cup tequila

¹/₄ cup orange liqueur (such as Cointreau, Grand Marnier, or triple sec)

¹/₄ cup sugar, or 3 tablespoons raw agave nectar

¹/₂ tablespoons Sriracha

Juice of 3 limes

Ice cubes or cold water as needed

Kosher salt or margarita salt, for rimming

Fresh mint leaves, for garnish

In a blender, combine the mango, orange juice, tequila, orange liqueur, sugar, Sriracha, and the juice of 2 of the limes. Blend until smooth. Add ice cubes or cold water to bring the volume up to 4 cups, choosing ice cubes for a thicker consistency and cold water for a thinner consistency. You may want to add the ice or water gradually so you can assess the consistency along the way.

Put the juice from the third lime in a shallow dish wide enough to accommodate the rim of the serving glasses. Put the salt in a separate shallow dish of similar size. Rim each glass first with lime juice, then with salt. Divide the margarita evenly among the glasses. Garnish with mint leaves and serve immediately.

> **OVER THE TOP TIP** For added zing, rim your glass with Sriracha Salt (page 49).

SUPER SIMPLE PEANUT BUTTER AND SRIRACHA COOKIES

A while back, I came across a recipe for peanut butter and Sriracha cookies on TheSugarPixie.net, and I kicked myself for not thinking of it first! I made them and fell in love instantly. Since then, I've played around with the recipe, and this version is my favorite: an incredibly simple adaptation that gets its sweetness from maple syrup, stays incredibly ooey-gooey, and won't hang around your kitchen very long at all. Especially if you use them to make ridiculously good ice cream sandwiches!

MAKES ABOUT 24 COOKIES

- 1 tablespoon ground flaxseeds
- 3 tablespoons water
- 1 cup natural creamy peanut butter, stirred well
- $1/3$ cup Grade B maple syrup
- 2 tablespoons Sriracha
- $1/4$ teaspoon fine sea salt
- $1/4$ teaspoon baking powder
- $1/4$ teaspoon baking soda

Preheat the oven to 350°F. Line a large baking sheet with parchment paper or a silicone mat.

In a small bowl, mix the flaxseeds and water and let sit for several minutes, until a gel forms. In a medium bowl, mix the flax gel, peanut butter, maple syrup, Sriracha, salt, baking powder, and baking soda. (The dough will be more moist and sticky than typical cookie dough, but it works out great!)

Drop heaping tablespoonfuls of the dough on the prepared baking sheet, spacing them about $1^1/2$ inches apart. Bake for 8 to 10 minutes, until lightly golden. Let cool on the pan for 15 minutes. Transfer to a wire cooling rack and let cool to room temperature.

> **SRIRACHOCOHOLIC VERSION** Need to feed your chocolate fix? Mix $1/2$ cup vegan chocolate chips or carob chips into the dough before baking.

PUMPKIN-SRIRACHA CHEEZECAKE WITH CHOCOLATE-PECAN CRUST

To anyone who thinks a vegan cheezecake can't be good, I assure you that you've never had one done right. This one will send your tongue into the stratosphere! Oh, and you don't mind that there's absolutely *no baking* involved, do you? Didn't think so. **MAKES 6 TO 8 SERVINGS**

Crust

8 pitted Medjool dates, soaked in cold water for 2 hours

2 cups raw pecan halves

3 tablespoons unsweetened cacao powder

$^1/_4$ teaspoon ground flaxseeds (optional)

$^1/_4$ teaspoon cloves

$^1/_8$ teaspoon fine sea salt

Filling

2 cups raw whole cashews, soaked in cold water for 4 hours

1 (15-ounce) can pumpkin puree

$^1/_2$ cup sugar

$^1/_4$ cup coconut oil

2 tablespoons Sriracha

2 teaspoons ground cinnamon

1 teaspoon vanilla extract

$^1/_2$ teaspoon ground ginger

$^1/_4$ teaspoon fine sea salt

Pecan halves, for decoration

Whipped coconut crème, for garnish (optional; see sidebar)

To make the crust, drain the dates. Put them in a food processor and add the pecans, cacao powder, flaxseeds, cloves, and salt. Process until a dough ball starts to form and pulls away from the sides of the bowl, about 2 minutes. Don't overmix, or the pecans will turn into nut butter. Lightly spritz an 8-inch springform pan or standard pie tin with nonstick cooking spray. Transfer the pecan mixture to the pan. If using a springform pan, press it in an even layer over the bottom of the pan. If using a standard pie tin, press it over the bottom and up the sides. Refrigerate while you prepare the filling.

To make the filling, drain the cashews. Put them in a food processor and add the pumpkin, sugar, oil, Sriracha, cinnamon, vanilla, ginger, and salt. Process until smooth.

To assemble the cheezecake, use a rubber spatula to spread the filling in an even layer over the crust and smooth the top. Place pecan halves around the perimeter, facing in, to decorate. Cover with plastic wrap and refrigerate until set, at least 4 hours. Before releasing from the springform pan, run a knife around the edge to aid with removal. (If using a standard pie tin, simply slice and serve directly from the pan.) Serve immediately, garnished with a dollop of whipped coconut crème. Leftovers (ha!) can be stored in the refrigerator for up to 1 week or in the freezer for up to 6 months.

WHIP IT! WHIP IT GOOD! Ever made whipped coconut crème? It's super easy to do. Refrigerate 1 (14-ounce) can of coconut milk (*not* the low-fat or light variety) for at least 4 hours. Open the can and scoop out all the creamy goodness that's solidified in there, leaving any liquid behind in the can. Using an electric hand mixer or a stand mixer fitted with the whisk attachment, beat the cream until light and fluffy, with soft peaks, about 4 minutes. Taste and sweeten with a touch of sugar or stevia and flavor with vanilla extract if desired. Stored in the refrigerator, it will keep for 2 days.

UPSIDE-DOWN PINEAPPLE-SRIRACHA CAKE

Oh, you poor maraschino cherry, what hath the modern food industry done to you? While I *love* your original liqueur-soaked incarnation, the syrupy neon garbage that you've become is atrocious. If only there were something else with a vibrant red hue that could look and taste nice in the center of the pineapple rings atop this upside-down cake . . . **MAKES 8 TO 12 SERVINGS**

1 (20-ounce) can pineapple slices packed in juice

¹/₄ cup light brown sugar

2 cups all-purpose flour

¹/₂ cup granulated sugar

1 teaspoon baking soda

1 teaspoon ground cinnamon

¹/₂ teaspoon fine sea salt

¹/₄ teaspoon baking powder

¹/₄ teaspoon ground cloves

¹/₂ cup unsweetened applesauce

1 tablespoon ground flaxseeds

1 tablespoon apple cider vinegar

Sriracha, for garnish

Preheat the oven to 350°F. Spray the bottom and sides of a 9-inch round cake pan or springform pan with nonstick cooking spray. Line the bottom with parchment paper and spray again.

Drain the pineapple, reserving the juice. Lay the pineapple slices in a single layer on a clean kitchen towel or paper towels. Cover with an additional towel or more paper towels and pat dry. Arrange some of the pineapple slices in a single layer in the prepared pan. Cut the remaining slices into chunks and place them in the spaces between the slices, leaving the holes in the center of the rings empty. Spread the brown sugar evenly over the pineapple.

In a bowl, mix the flour, granulated sugar, baking soda, cinnamon, salt, baking powder, and cloves. In a separate bowl, mix ³/₄ cup of the reserved juice with the applesauce, flaxseeds, and vinegar. Let sit for 2 minutes. Add to the dry ingredients and stir just until combined. Pour over the pineapple and place in the oven immediately.

CONTINUED

Bake for about 30 minutes, until the cake is set and a toothpick inserted in the center comes out clean. Let cool to room temperature in the pan. Run a knife around the sides, invert a serving plate over the pan, and flip them over to turn the cake out onto the plate. Squirt a thin layer of Sriracha over the holes in the pineapple rings to loosely resemble typical, loathsome maraschino cherries. Cut into slices, let diners admire the novelty, then recommend that they spread the Sriracha over their piece before enjoying so the heat isn't all packed into one bite. Covered and stored at room temperature, leftovers will keep for 2 days.

GF For the all-purpose flour, use your favorite gluten-free flour or baking mix. (If the baking mix already contains salt, baking powder, and/or baking soda, omit those ingredients when mixing the cake batter.)

MAPLE-SRIRACHA DOUGHNUTS

Not too long ago, my buddies from the New Brew Thursday podcast invited me to appear on their show to talk Sriracha. On the set, I saw a pink box (the universal sign for doughnuts), I reached in, grabbed a maple bar, topped it with Sriracha, and blew their minds. Then, my buddy/beer pairing expert "Dr." Bill Sysak matched it up with a holiday beer called Our Special Ale from Anchor Brewing in San Francisco, and blew *my* mind. It was a good day. Now I'm taking the doughnut idea one step further and incorporating the Sriracha into the icing. One heads-up: You'll need two doughnut pans with six cavities each for this recipe. **MAKES 12 DOUGHNUTS**

Doughnuts

- 2 tablespoons ground flaxseeds
- 6 tablespoons water
- 1^1/$_2$ cups all-purpose flour
- ^{3}/$_1$ cup sugar
- 1^1/$_2$ teaspoons baking powder
- ^{1}/$_2$ teaspoon ground ginger
- ^{1}/$_2$ teaspoon ground cinnamon
- ^{1}/$_2$ teaspoon fine sea salt
- ^{1}/$_4$ teaspoon baking soda
- ^{2}/$_3$ cup unsweetened almond milk
- ^{1}/$_3$ cup coconut oil, melted
- ^{3}/$_4$ teaspoon apple cider vinegar

Icing

- ^{3}/$_4$ cup sifted confectioners' sugar
- 2 tablespoons Grade B maple syrup
- 2 tablespoons Sriracha
- 1 to 2 tablespoons unsweetened almond milk

To make the doughnuts, mix the flaxseeds and water in a small bowl and let sit for several minutes, until a gel forms.

Preheat the oven to 350°F. In a large bowl, mix the flour, sugar, baking powder, ginger, cinnamon, salt, and baking soda. In a small bowl, mix the almond milk, oil, and vinegar. Add to the flour mixture and stir until combined. Transfer the batter to two nonstick doughnut pans, dividing it evenly among them.

Bake for 12 to 15 minutes, until a toothpick inserted in a doughnut comes out clean. Invert onto a cooling rack set over a baking sheet and let cool to room temperature.

To make the icing, combine the sugar, maple syrup, Sriracha, and 1 tablespoon of the almond milk and whisk until well

CONTINUED

blended. The icing should be somewhat thick, but still fluid enough to coat the doughnuts evenly when they're dipped in. Add up to 1 tablespoon more almond milk if necessary.

Sweep the doughnuts through the icing to coat the top half of each, then put them back on the cooling rack, icing side up, and let sit until the icing is firm, about 10 minutes.

GF For the all-purpose flour, use your favorite gluten-free flour or baking mix. (If the baking mix already contains salt, baking powder, and/or baking soda, omit those ingredients when mixing the doughnut batter.)

INDEX

In loving memory of
Nana Norma, Papa Dave, Uncle Dave,
Aunt Ginny, Uncle Len, and Nana Nancy

Library of Congress Cataloging-in-
Publication Data is on file with the publisher

Hardcover ISBN: 978-1-60774-460-3
eBook ISBN: 978-1-60774-461-0

Printed in China

Design by Chloe Rawlins
Food styling by Karen Shinto
Prop styling by Carol Hacker
Photography assisting by Amanda Hibbert
and Agustina Peretta

10 9 8 7 6 5 4 3 2 1

First Edition

MEASUREMENT CONVERSION CHART

VOLUME

US	IMPERIAL	METRIC
1 tablespoon	$\frac{1}{2}$ fl oz	15 ml
2 tablespoons	1 fl oz	30 ml
$\frac{1}{4}$ cup	2 fl oz	60 ml
$\frac{1}{3}$ cup	3 fl oz	90 ml
$\frac{1}{2}$ cup	4 fl oz	120 ml
$\frac{2}{3}$ cup	5 fl oz ($\frac{1}{4}$ pint)	150 ml
$\frac{3}{4}$ cup	6 fl oz	180 ml
1 cup	8 fl oz ($\frac{1}{3}$ pint)	240 ml
$1\frac{1}{4}$ cups	10 fl oz ($\frac{1}{2}$ pint)	300 ml
2 cups (1 pint)	16 fl oz ($\frac{2}{3}$ pint)	480 ml
$2\frac{1}{2}$ cups	20 fl oz (1 pint)	600 ml
1 quart	32 fl oz ($1\frac{2}{3}$ pints)	1 l

TEMPERATURE

FAHRENHEIT	CELSIUS/GAS MARK
250°F	120°C/gas mark $\frac{1}{2}$
275°F	135°C/gas mark 1
300°F	150°C/gas mark 2
325°F	160°C/gas mark 3
350°F	175 or 180°C/gas mark 4
375°F	190°C/gas mark 5
400°F	200°C/gas mark 6
425°F	220°C/gas mark 7
450°F	230°C/gas mark 8
475°F	245°C/gas mark 9
500°F	260°C

LENGTH

INCH	METRIC
$\frac{1}{4}$ inch	6 mm
$\frac{1}{2}$ inch	1.25 cm
$\frac{3}{4}$ inch	2 cm
1 inch	2.5 cm
6 inches ($\frac{1}{2}$ foot)	15 cm
12 inches (1 foot)	30 cm

WEIGHT

US/IMPERIAL	METRIC
$\frac{1}{2}$ oz	15 g
1 oz	30 g
2 oz	60 g
$\frac{1}{4}$ lb	115 g
$\frac{1}{3}$ lb	150 g
$\frac{1}{2}$ lb	225 g
$\frac{3}{4}$ lb	350 g
1 lb	450 g